Language Teaching:
A Scheme for Teacher Education

Editors: C N Candlin and H G Widdowson

Pronunciation

Christiane Dalton and Barbara Seidlhofer

WITHDRAWN

Oxford University Press

Oxford University Press
Walton Street, Oxford OX2 6DP

Oxford New York
Athens Auckland Bangkok Bombay
Calcutta Cape Town Dar es Salaam Delhi
Florence Hong Kong Istanbul Karachi
Kuala Lumpur Madras Madrid Melbourne
Mexico City Nairobi Paris Singapore
Taipei Tokyo Toronto

and associated companies in
Berlin Ibadan

OXFORD and OXFORD ENGLISH
are trade marks of Oxford University Press

ISBN 0 19 437197 2

© Oxford University Press 1994

First published 1994
Second impression 1995

No unauthorized photocopying

All rights reserved. No part of this publication may be reproduced, stored
in a retrieval system, or transmitted, in any form or by any means,
electronic, mechanical, photocopying, recording, or otherwise, without
the prior written permission of Oxford University Press.

This book is sold subject to the condition that it shall not, by way of
trade or otherwise, be lent, re-sold, hired out, or otherwise circulated
without the publisher's prior consent in any form of binding or cover
other than that in which it is published and without a similar condition
including this condition being imposed on the subsequent purchaser.

Set by Wyvern Typesetting Ltd, Bristol

Printed in Hong Kong

To Henry Widdowson
and
to Stephanie

Contents

The authors and series editors

Barbara Seidlhofer read English and Italian at Vienna University. She qualified as a secondary school teacher and went on to read applied linguistics at London University. She holds an MA and a PhD in applied linguistics from London University and has taught German in the UK. She currently works as a researcher and lecturer in linguistics and methodology at the English Department of Vienna University.

Christiane Dalton is a graduate of Vienna University where she read English, Spanish, and history. She qualified as a secondary school teacher and holds a PhD in English linguistics. She has taught German in the UK and currently works as a researcher and lecturer in linguistics and phonetics at the English Department of Vienna University.

Christopher N. Candlin is Professor of Linguistics in the School of English and Linguistics at Macquarie University, Sydney, and Executive Director of the National Centre for English Language Teaching and Research, having previously been Professor of Applied Linguistics and Director of the Centre for Language in Social Life at the University of Lancaster. He also co-founded and directed the Institute for English Language Education at Lancaster.

Henry Widdowson is Professor of English for Speakers of Other Languages at the University of London Institute of Education, and Professor of Applied Linguistics at the University of Essex. He was previously Lecturer in Applied Linguistics at the University of Edinburgh, and has also worked as an English Language Officer for the British Council in Sri Lanka and Bangladesh.

Through work with The British Council, The Council of Europe, and other agencies, both Editors have had extensive and varied experience of language teaching, teacher education, and curriculum development overseas, and both contribute to seminars, conferences, and professional journals.

Introduction

Pronunciation

Over recent years there has been renewed interest in the teaching of pronunciation which has resulted in a bewildering variety of new teaching materials being published. How, then, is the teacher to know which ones to use? This book aims to equip teachers with the necessary background knowledge and a rationale for applying this knowledge to principled decisions about their own classroom situation.

Pronunciation is never an end in itself but a means to negotiate meaning in discourse, and this is what guided the selection of aspects covered. This book is thus not intended as a full-blown introduction to phonetics, but aims to provide a frame of reference which enables teachers to relate the 'what' and 'how' of their actual teaching to the 'why'.

What teachers need to know is not necessarily what learners need to learn. We believe that there is an important distinction to be made between what is important for the teacher in training and what is useful for learners in the classroom. We have emphasized this distinction by arranging the contents of Sections One and Two in reverse order: bottom-up in Section One and top-down in Section Two. While teacher education may require an understanding of pronunciation as an aspect of the language system, it will often be preferable in teaching to proceed according to priorities determined by how pronunciation functions in language use.

Section One introduces the main concepts and terminology of the field. Section Two then invites readers to reflect upon and evaluate activities from published materials with reference to these concepts. Section Three offers tasks for testing out ideas and insights from Sections One and Two against the reality of the classroom.

In principle, the points made in this book apply to the pronunciation of any language. But as this book is written in English and this is therefore the only language shared by all readers, most examples and illustrations refer to English.

Whatever the language in question, our hope is that the insights gained from working through this book will equip teachers with relevant points of reference. What are needed, it seems to us, are models to approximate to rather than norms to imitate. Knowledge about discourse tells us that appropriacy is a more important criterion for intelligibility than correctness. This view accordingly shifts the emphasis away from native speakers as yardsticks of 'correctness' to teachers taking informed decisions as to what is desirable and feasible in order to meet the needs of specific learners.

We would like to thank several people for their help and support. Our students at Vienna University have over many years shaped our awareness of the complexities and sensitivities involved in pronunciation teaching. Ilse Schindler was an ideal combination of a sympathetic and critical reader. Our colleagues Herbert Schendl and Gunther Kaltenböck also made valuable comments on earlier drafts, and Keith Chester helped with the proof-reading. Harald Mittermann, our librarian, kept us abreast of a wealth of new publications, pointing out his latest acquisitions. The IATEFL PronSIG has offered a stimulating environment of fellow enthusiasts and Jonathan Marks kept an eye on our Finnish and Polish examples. Anne Conybeare and Julia Sallabank at OUP were very supportive editors and mended many a loophole in our manuscript. Christopher Candlin provided constructive criticism. And Nobody selflessly relieved us from all the domestic chores and typed the manuscript from our illegible scribble.

There is one person who deserves a separate paragraph: Henry Widdowson. His generosity in sharing his time and ideas with us, his Socratic gift of persistently asking the right questions have shaped this book and given us inspiration and confidence.

Barbara Seidlhofer
Christiane Dalton

Language Teaching:
A Scheme for Teacher Education

The purpose of this scheme of books is to engage language teachers in a process of continual professional development. We have designed it so as to guide teachers towards the critical appraisal of ideas and the informed application of these ideas in their own classrooms. The scheme provides the means for teachers to take the initiative themselves in pedagogic planning. The emphasis is on critical enquiry as a basis for effective action.

We believe that advances in language teaching stem from the independent efforts of teachers in their own classrooms. This independence is not brought about by imposing fixed ideas and promoting fashionable formulas. It can only occur where teachers, individually or collectively, explore principles and experiment with techniques. Our purpose is to offer guidance on how this might be achieved.

The scheme consists of three sub-series of books covering areas of enquiry and practice of immediate relevance to language teaching and learning. Sub-series 1 (of which this present volume forms a part) focuses on areas of *language knowledge*, with books linked to the conventional levels of linguistic description: pronunciation, vocabulary, grammar, and discourse. Sub-series 2 focuses on different *modes of behaviour* which realize this knowledge. It is concerned with the pedagogic skills of speaking, listening, reading, and writing. Sub-series 3 focuses on a variety of *modes of action* which are needed if this knowledge and behaviour is to be acquired in the operation of language teaching. The books in this sub-series have to do with such topics as syllabus design, the content of language courses, and aspects of methodology and evaluation.

This sub-division of the field is not meant to suggest that different topics can be dealt with in isolation. On the contrary, the concept of a scheme implies making coherent links between all these different areas of enquiry and activity. We wish to emphasize how their integration formalizes the complex factors present in any teaching process. Each book, then, highlights a particular topic, but also deals contingently with other issues, themselves treated as focal in other books in the series. Clearly, an enquiry into a mode of behaviour like speaking, for example, must also refer to aspects of language knowledge which it realizes. It must also connect to modes of action which can be directed at developing this behaviour in learners. As elements of the whole scheme, therefore, books cross-refer both within and across the different sub-series.

This principle of cross-reference which links the elements of the scheme is also applied to the internal design of the different inter-related books within it. Thus, each book contains three sections, which, by a combination of text and task, engage the reader in a principled enquiry into ideas and practices. The first section of each book makes explicit those theoretical ideas which bear on the topic in question. It provides a conceptual framework for those sections which follow. Here the text has a mainly *explanatory* function, and the tasks serve to clarify and consolidate the points raised. The second section shifts the focus of attention to how the ideas from Section One relate to activities in the classroom. Here the text is concerned with *demonstration*, and the tasks are designed to get teachers to evaluate suggestions for teaching in reference both to the ideas from Section One and also to their own teaching experience. In the third section this experience is projected into future work. Here the set of tasks, modelled on those on Section Two, is designed to be carried out by the reader as a combination of teaching techniques and action research in the actual classroom. It is this section that renews the reader's contact with reality: the ideas expounded in Section One and linked to pedagogic practice in Section Two are now to be systematically *tested out* in the process of classroom teaching.

If language teaching is to be a genuinely professional enterprise, it requires continual experimentation and evaluation on the part of practitioners whereby in seeking to be more effective in their pedagogy they provide at the same time—and as a corollary—for their own continuing education. It is our aim in this scheme to promote this dual purpose.

Christopher N. Candlin
Henry Widdowson

Explanation

1 The significance of pronunciation

We can define pronunciation in general terms as the production of significant sound in two senses.

First, sound is significant because it is used as part of a code of a particular language. So we can talk about the distinctive sounds of English, French, Thai, and other languages. In this sense we can talk about pronunciation as the production and reception of sounds of speech.

Second, sound is significant because it is used to achieve meaning in contexts of use. Here the code combines with other factors to make communication possible. In this sense we can talk about pronunciation with reference to acts of speaking.

In this book we shall consider pronunciation in both senses. But we shall give particular prominence to communicative aspects, and refer to the physical features of sound only in so far as they are relevant to an understanding of how they figure in discourse, that is to say in the achievement of meaning. We begin with general points about the role of pronunciation in social interaction.

1.1 Pronunciation and identity

As human beings we are individuals, but at the same time we are also members of groups. By almost everything we do, we simultaneously express ourselves and relate to others, either consciously or unconsciously. Both these aspects are important for establishing what we are and who we are; in short, for establishing our identity.

▶ TASK 1

If you are working on your own, go straight to the second part of the task.

1 Look at the person next to you for one minute. Do not say anything. Now jot down what you think has been communicated to you and how. Then take a few minutes to discuss with your partner whether the 'messages' you got were correct.

2 Look at yourself in a full-size mirror (or in your mind's eye) and consider what in your appearance today represents a deliberate

attempt to convey a particular message about yourself.
(adapted from Ellis and McClintock 1990: 35ff.)

It is astonishing how much information we get about others simply by taking in a person's facial expression, posture, and of course the clothes they wear. In many societies clothes can be a powerful and versatile means of communicating something about the wearer.

Something very similar happens in language and speech: into the perfectly neutral transaction of purchasing a theatre ticket, we manage to pack a wealth of information about ourselves. We are likely to give away our sex and approximate age, of course, but from our experience as listeners we know that our interlocutors may also be making judgements about where we come from, what social class we belong to, our educational status, and whether we are generally a likeable person or not.

There is evidence that even the disembodied voice can convey not only indications of social, but also of individual identity, as when we build up a picture of people we only know from their voices on the telephone or radio.

▶ **TASK 2**

In experiments to test people's reactions to different voices and accents, subjects are commonly asked to listen to a tape with samples and to indicate their impressions on scales which include opposites such as the following:

1 interesting_____boring
2 brave _____cowardly
3 kind _____cruel
4 friendly_____unfriendly
5 old _____young

Since we have no tape available here, we might attempt the reverse procedure: imagine you are an actor who has been asked to impersonate the above characteristics by saying the sentence 'I suppose I could do it' (or something similar in your own language). How do you vary your voice in order to convey characteristics (1) to (5) and their opposites? If you have the opportunity to work in pairs, get your partner to listen to you; if not, listen to a recording.

In order to convey the characteristics suggested in this task, it is likely that you varied the quality and pitch of your voice, the speed of your speech, and maybe your accent. You may also have been conscious of calling to mind your personal experience with specific people; our judgements of the way people 'sound' are based on a combination of individual and social criteria.

When we learn our native language we do not only acquire the code and its variations; we also learn to make value judgements about the use of these different forms—we acquire a complex system of social meanings. We may even try to present ourselves as members of a group we do not really belong to, but which we would like to be associated with. As our most complex signalling system, spoken language is particularly versatile in this respect.

Our reaction to the social meaning of a form is very often transferred to the form itself. For instance, we frequently perceive a certain speech sound as either beautiful or vulgar without taking into account that the sound in itself can be neither. Take the *diphthong* [aɪ]: in Britain it is commonly regarded as neutral if it is part of the word 'pint', but some people would think it ugly or vulgar if it occurred (as in Cockney speech) in a realization of 'paint'. (For transcription symbols and conventions see the Appendix, pages 172–3.)

▶ # TASK 3

Can you think of another example? From another language or across languages? Do you, for instance, happen to know how the song 'The rain in Spain' from *My Fair Lady* has been translated into other languages?

In the English original, Eliza's problem is that she is using the Cockney dipthong [aɪ] ([raɪn, spaɪn]) whereas Professor Higgins insists on the Standard [eɪ]. In the German translation, 'Es grünt so grün, wenn Spaniens Blüten blühen', Eliza says [griːn] and [bliːtn] for [gryːn] and [blyːtn], which is regarded as typical of Berlin working class speech.

In making these value judgements, we show that we know not only the language, but also something about the society in which it is used. On linguistic grounds alone, we would not be able to tell whether a certain linguistic form is prestigious or not. Linguists have therefore tried to develop terms which allow us talk about these issues objectively.

Distinctions within the code of a language in general are called *varieties*. Regional varieties which differ from the common core with respect to syntax, lexicon, morphology, and phonology are called *dialects*. Regional and/or social varieties which only differ with respect to phonology (sound level) have been termed *accents*. Thus, the speech of newsreaders on American, British, and Australian TV is likely to be the same dialect, i.e. Standard English, but different in terms of accent.

Variation in accent has not only a regional but also a social dimension, and is therefore also related to prestige. On the whole, prestige varieties tend to be more geographically neutral than non-prestige ones (as illustrated, for instance, by the pronunciation of many newsreaders on national radio and television). However, the exact interdependence of geographical and social factors varies among speech communities. British society seems to exploit differences in accent as social markers to a greater extent than American society, for instance. This probably explains why the prestige variety of British English (or, as Trudgill and Hannah (1985) point out, 'English English') is so well documented that it is the best described phonetic variety of any language on earth. This is also the reason why we draw on it more extensively here than on *General American*. Although much the same points could be made about that or any other prestige variety, it does seem as if people are particularly sensitive about the issue of *RP*. (Terms in italics are explained in the Glossary, page 174.)

The term RP is customarily used to describe prestige 'English English' and stands for 'Received Pronunciation'. This name indicates that it is essentially a social variety. And indeed, although its historical roots lie in the south-east of England, it is used by speakers to express a certain social identity. There have been numerous studies among speakers of other English accents in order to find out which values they connect with RP. Not surprisingly, it has turned out that they are the same as the values perceived as necessary for socio-economic success: intelligence, professional competence, persuasive power, diligence, social privilege, etc. On the other hand, RP speakers are also perceived as distant, unfriendly, arrogant, and even dishonest (Hudson 1980: chapter 6).

When it comes to language teaching, it is important to note that there is a difference between what is effective as a point of reference or set of bearings for learning (let us call this a model) and what is presented as an attainable behavioural target (let us call this a norm). The task of pronunciation teaching, as in the teaching of any other aspect of language, is (in these terms) to establish models for guidance, not norms for imitation.

Why, then, do we use a prestige form such as RP as a model for foreign learners? Do we want them to make a bid for membership of the privileged speaker group?

▶ **TASK 4**

What accent—if any in particular—do you use as a model for teaching? If it is RP, can you think of any reasons other than tradition?

The argument usually put forward for using a prestige accent such as RP as a model is that it is easy to get information about it, as it is the most fully described accent. John Wells calls a 'redefined RP', which takes account of recent changes documented by him, 'the only practical pronunciation model for the Br[itish] E[nglish]-oriented EFL learner' (1991: 108). Another argument is that prestige forms tend to be more widely accepted in a wider range of communicative situations, while non-prestige accents are often regarded as 'odd' or idiosyncratic.

However, as we have indicated, language is used not only to communicate, but also to establish a sense of community. Consequently, we need to ask ourselves to what extent learners need, or indeed want, to join the native-speaker community. Being recognizable as a foreigner to our interlocutors suspends the automatic judgements carried out within their routine value system. A foreign accent can place the learner outside the power game in the native-speaker community, and may therefore be an asset rather than a handicap.

On the other hand, power is not the only defining characteristic of social relations. There is also solidarity. By adapting his or her accent to that of the native-speaker community, the learner may express solidarity with that community. The motivation for this may be integrative if the learner wishes to be accepted by the native-speaker community as an 'honorary member'. Adapting one's accent can, however, have instrumental pay-offs as well: if people recognize you as a member of their group they might be more ready to help you than if you are an outsider.

However, there are also possible penalties for approximating too closely to the pronunciation of the native-speaker community. Its members may think that you are claiming membership without being properly qualified. In this case, you may find yourself resented as an intruder who is claiming solidarity without warrant.

Furthermore, it may be seen as objectionable to oblige learners to conform to an alien code of conduct. It may even be seen as forcing them to reject their own identity. Pronunciation is so much a matter of self-image that students may prefer to keep their accent deliberately, in order to retain their self-respect or to gain the approval of their peers.

Thus, Porter and Garvin (1989) say that the following two statements about attitudes towards the teaching of pronunciation are regularly expressed by teachers:

'By requiring someone to utter strange sounds, etc. we are making them go against deeply rooted conceptions of what is desirable, correct, acceptable, dignified, etc. The teaching of pronunciation will therefore go against the grain, and may even constitute a humiliation.

... A person's pronunciation is one expression of that person's self-image. To seek to change someone's pronunciation—whether of the L1 or of an L2—is to tamper with their self-image, and is thus unethical—morally wrong.'
(Porter and Garvin 1989: 8)

▶ TASK 5

Do you agree with either of these statements? If you do, what do you think you should do as a teacher to counter the effects that Porter and Garvin refer to?

Porter and Garvin conclude from their findings, which are based on questionnaires, that 'learners should be given what they want, which underlines the necessity to find out what they want' (1989:15).

Giving learners what they want may not always be possible or desirable, but it is obvious that their attitudes should be taken into account in pronunciation, as in other aspects of language.

So insisting on 'correct' pronunciation may not always be desirable. And it may not be feasible, either. People invest so much of their identity in the way they speak that their pronunciation frequently proves extremely resistant to change, particularly with older learners. There is a good deal of evidence that *early* language learning is an advantage, especially in the domain of pronunciation. Suggested explanations have included the 'plasticity' of the young brain and 'lateralization', i.e. the claim that the two brain hemispheres are not specialized, or lateralized, before adolescence. Even studies that are very careful to point out the cognitive advantages which older learners may have over younger ones concede that children are probably better at acquiring an acceptable accent than adults. There is no one age which is ideal for all aspects involved in language learning (see, for example, Ellis 1994: chapter 11 for a discussion of these issues).

A different explanation for the apparent advantage of early learning of the spoken language is Schumann's (1975) affective theory. He recognizes that individuals are also social beings, and argues that children's personalities are more permeable, both emotionally and socially, and thus more open to language influences than adolescents and adults.

Thus, while no age stands out as optimal for all aspects of foreign language learning, it has been established that due to certain psycho-sociological factors, our resistance to modifying our pronunciation increases as we get older: our ego-boundaries get established with age, our 'language ego' (Guiora, Brannon, and Dull 1972) becomes less flexible. Generally, our flexibility decreases as our investment in the linguistic expression of our identity increases. This means that the affective demands made upon an individual by language learning in general, and pronunciation in particular, can be considerable. Just how strongly these demands make themselves felt will depend on a combination of motivation, instructional situation, social attitudes, and personality factors such as extroversion/introversion, anxiety, and empathy.

Given the importance of affective and personality factors in foreign language learning, it is not surprising that so-called *fossilization* is a widespread phenomenon (Selinker 1992). There are many adults who speak a foreign language expertly, often because they have lived in the foreign language community for a long time. What is interesting for us here is that many of these people retain a distinct foreign accent with the phonetic characteristics of their first language.

We have argued that language variation is normal and, indeed, all-pervasive. We have seen how pronunciation is closely bound up with social and individual identity. People's accents express their membership of particular communities, and so also express such conflicting tendencies as power and solidarity, in-group and out-group, prestige and stigmatization. Pronunciation expresses a sense of individual identity as well. It reflects ego-boundaries which are extremely resistant to change. In short, particular ways of speaking can be seen as an investment in identity, and therefore careful consideration needs to be given to both the feasibility and the desirability of forcing learners into a mould of 'correct' pronunciation based on native-speaker norms.

However, we also need to recognize that there must be *some* model for learners to work towards.

1.2 Pronunciation and intelligibility

It is often said that what is important for learners is to acquire an accent which is 'intelligible', or to achieve 'comfortable intelligibility' (Kenworthy 1987: 3). In **1.1** we considered the crucial role that voice and accent play in our perception of ourselves and others, so it is likely that social and psychological factors also bear upon the question of intelligibility. Making yourself understood is not just a matter of accurate and clear articulation, and pronunciation cannot be considered or taught in isolation, dissociated from questions such as 'Why do we talk?', 'What determines how we talk to whom?', and 'Which factors might be of help or hindrance to getting our meaning across?'

The word 'meaning' in this last question deserves further consideration. When, for instance, we buy a train ticket with a long queue behind us, our main concern is to get across where we want to go and whether we require a single or a return ticket. The objective here is to achieve a transaction as efficiently as possible. The transaction will be regarded as successful if we get the ticket we want. There are, however, occasions where we talk for quite different reasons. Imagine you are at a reception and you have just started a conversation with a total stranger. The exchange of precise information may well be of very little importance here. You and your interlocutor are much more likely to focus on interaction and the way you project an image of yourselves. The success of this interaction is typically determined by whether you manage to keep the small talk going in an amicable atmosphere. The most satisfying outcome for the interlocutors is probably taking a liking to each other. (For the interaction/transaction distinction see Brown and Yule 1983: 1ff., and **3.2** below.)

Bearing in mind that no strict line can be drawn between transactional and interactional talk, we could say that the criteria as to what constitutes good, or successful, pronunciation will vary greatly between the two. The customer at the train station will fulfil his purpose if his request for a ticket is accessible (i.e. intelligible) to the clerk behind the counter—that is to say, if he is able to pronounce the name of his destination and something like 'day return' in such a way that the clerk can act upon it. Matters are more complicated for the people at the reception: they will have to accomplish more than mere accessibility in their utterances. In fact, since it is unlikely that really vital information will be expressed, it does not matter much if some words are not understood at all. What does matter is whether the people chat in such a way that they find each other acceptable (Widdowson 1984: 84ff.).

Both accessibility and acceptability are rather more complex than is immediately apparent from our simple examples. What makes them complex is, above all, that they cannot be fixed or defined in any absolute way, but depend on various, and variable, factors. Thus, whether an utterance is accessible or not will be determined not only by the accuracy and clarity of the speaker's enunciation, but also by the listener's expectation and attitude, such as experience with, and tolerance of, low prestige or foreign accents. On the other hand, whether the interlocutors find each others' pronunciation acceptable will largely depend on the value they attribute to each others' accents, and on whether they regard these as appropriate to the occasion and to their respective roles and status in society.

These factors can sometimes take on particular significance. Wolff (1964), for instance, describes the phenomenon of 'non-reciprocal' intelligibility. The Nembe and the Kalabari are two communities in the Eastern Niger Delta. The Kalabari are the largest and most prosperous group in the area, an 'up-and-coming' society. The Nembe, on the other hand, are the 'poor country cousins' without any economic and political power. The languages of the two communities are so similar that on the basis of linguistic comparison they could be regarded as dialects of the same language; the groups also inhabit geographically contiguous territories. Nevertheless, whereas the Nembe say that they can understand Kalabari, the Kalabari claim that Nembe is a different language unintelligible to them except for some words.

▶ # TASK 6

How does the situation described by Wolff relate to the criteria of accessibility and acceptability? Do you know of a situation similar to that of the Nembe and Kalabari which might be accounted for in the same way?

The point which we want to emphasize here is that intelligibility is by no means guaranteed by linguistic similarity and phonetic accuracy, but is often overridden by cultural and economic factors.

Intelligibility, therefore, is closely linked to the issues raised in **1.1**: social position and individual character. We adjust our understanding of the other person according to how we relate to them socially and as individuals.

As native speakers of our first language, we tend to deal with this complexity so automatically and with such ease that we are hardly aware of the innumerable factors which influence the way we talk to people. We automatically adapt our ways of speaking to situations and interlocutors. However, learning a foreign language may make us painfully aware of these factors.

This awareness will be affected by our purpose and motivation. In their classic study, Gardner and Lambert (1972) distinguish between instrumental and integrative motivation in second language learning. An instrumental orientation reflects the practical advantages of learning a language, while an integrative orientation stems from 'a sincere and personal interest in the people and the culture' (Gardner and Lambert 1972: 132). Obviously, this distinction is a very general one between two extreme positions, and many learners may actually go through different 'motivational stages' in their language learning career.

What interests us here is that there seems to be a relationship between kinds of motivation and the distinctions we have made above: a learner with primarily instrumental motivation will probably be interested mainly in getting meanings across, and regard his or her linguistic performance as satisfying if it is accessible to interlocutors. An integratively motivated learner, on the other hand, will probably set greater store by the interactional side of communication, and will be concerned to be not only accessible but also acceptable to the foreign language community he or she is aspiring to be a member of.

We are, of course, talking here about general orientations towards learning. Attitudes and motivation can naturally change, both in the course of learning and, indeed, in the course of a particular interaction. Nevertheless, as a kind of general guide for thinking about the goals of pronunciation teaching, it might be helpful to put the distinctions we have been making at the extreme points of a scale:

primary communicative goal	transaction _____	interaction
main criterion	accessibility _____	acceptability
motivation	instrumental _____	integrative
communication seen as	transmission _____	negotiation

▶   TASK 7

Consider the teaching situation you are involved in. Decide where on the above continuum you would place the goals and priorities of your teaching.

Wherever you may have placed *your* priorities, the point we should like to make in this book is that it is a matter of local decision as to what is suitable in specific situations. If we reflect upon how pronunciation works to make communication possible, we do not need to rely primarily on native speakers as models and arbiters of 'correctness'; we can use our own knowledge and awareness to decide in individual cases which criteria are crucial for achieving intelligibility. Hence, the relevant question to ask is not: what is *correct* in relation to a native-speaker norm (RP or otherwise), but: what is *appropriate* and necessary to be able to communicate in specific situations?

The purpose of this book is to highlight the factors which need to be involved in making a decision about the pronunciation to be taught, so that individuals can then decide in a principled way what they need, and *choose* how far they want to strive towards a native-speaker norm (an extremely elusive concept in itself). This would, of course, also allow for the choice not to worry about a distinct foreign accent.

2 The nature of speech sounds

We use our bodies to communicate with others. We may use our whole body to express something, such as facing (or facing away from) someone, or bowing or standing up to show respect. We may use parts of the body, as when we make gestures with our hands, or produce facial expressions. But the most subtle use we make of our bodies in producing sounds is with our organs of speech.

2.1 Sounds in the body

Sounds are fundamental to us. Even the unborn child picks up, and reacts to, sounds within and outside the womb, such as the mother's heartbeat, music, or voices. A baby can hear (and indeed be heard) long before it can see properly. Our speech organs, however, are not primarily organs for producing sounds. They are, first and foremost, involved in such life-supporting functions as breathing and eating. Thus, life and sounds are inextricably tied together.

▶ **TASK 8**

This is best done in pairs. If you are on your own, it would be good if you could observe yourself in a mirror. First, think of a simple narrative, for instance 'How I started the day today'. Now try and relate this to your partner, or to yourself in the mirror, *without* moving anything other than your speech organs—no smile, no gestures, no eye movement. If you have a listener, ask him or her *not* to give you any feedback signals—no nodding, smiling, 'mhm', or 'yes'!

You probably found this task very difficult and unnatural—maybe you felt like a robot. This is because acts of speech are physical acts which often involve the whole body. Nobody talks by simply moving their speech organs: eye movement, mime, and gesture are usually involved as well. Thus, we use the body to accompany sound, not just to produce sound. As Abercrombie (1972: 64) puts it, 'we speak with our vocal organs, but we converse with our entire bodies'. A telling example of this is the expressive use of mime and gesture by people conversing in sign language, which even allows non-signing people to guess at what they are saying.

How, then, do we use our bodies to produce the sounds that make up language?

▶ TASK 9

How many similarities can you list between the way a wind instrument produces music and the way we produce speech sounds?

To start with, we need energy, usually in the form of breath from the lungs, and speech organs with moveable parts, such as lips and tongue. The shape of the vocal tract (pharynx, oral cavity, nasal cavity) determines the quality of speech sounds through various modifications of the airstream.

The most general distinction between different speech sounds is that between *vowels* and *consonants*. During the articulation of vowels, the air flows freely out of the mouth. When the airstream is obstructed somewhere in the vocal tract, either partially or completely, we produce consonants.

Exploring the articulation of consonants and vowels

We can begin with a few experiments in order to observe how our articulatory organs function in producing speech sounds. Consonants first:

▶ TASK 10

Prepare to pronounce a [p] as in 'pot', but do not actually say anything. Just let as much pressure build up in your mouth as you can. Which parts of your mouth do most of the work in holding back the air pressure? And consequently, which parts do you move to release the pressure when finally saying the [p]?

It is easy to identify both lips as the articulating organs. When the lips part rapidly, this results in the release of the compressed air which is like an explosion. This is why [p] is called a *bilabial plosive*. Because [p] is pronounced with considerable breath effort and muscular energy, it is called a strong, or *fortis*, bilabial plosive, as opposed to [b], which, while being articulated in the same manner, is a relatively weak, or *lenis*, bilabial plosive. In most cases, the vocal cords vibrate during the articulation of [b], [d], and [g], which is why they are also described as voiced, whereas [p], [t], and [k] are voiceless.

Instead of using the lips for forming a closure, plosives can also be articulated with the tip of the tongue against the teeth ridge (or *alveolar* ridge) ([t], [d]), and between the back of the tongue and the soft palate, or *velum*, which will result in the velar plosives [k] or [g].

▶ **TASK 11**

Say a long [f] as in 'feel', or a succession of 'f's: [ffffff]. Where do you feel the airstream passing through? Can you produce a lenis variant of [f]?

As opposed to [p] and [b], which are pronounced by releasing air from the mouth cavity in a kind of explosion, [f] and its lenis counterpart [v] are continuous sounds. They are articulated by the inside of the lower lip making light contact with the upper teeth, so that the escaping air produces friction. This is why they are called *labio-dental fricatives*.

One more category of consonant:

▶ **TASK 12**

Pronounce the sounds [m] and [n] in alteration: m n m n m n

What do they have in common? What are the differences between them?

For both [m] and [n], a closure is made in the mouth. The airstream escapes through the nose in both cases, and both sounds are *voiced* (i.e. your vocal cords vibrate, as you can feel when you touch your Adam's apple). However, for the articulation of [m] we need both lips to form a closure, while for [n] the closure is formed with the tongue against the teeth ridge (or alveolar ridge) and upper side teeth. In other words, [m] is a *bilabial nasal* and [n] an *alveolar nasal*.

Summing up, we can say that there are three main criteria for describing consonants:

- *place of articulation*: where the airstream gets obstructed
- *manner of articulation*: how the airstream gets obstructed
- *force of articulation*: with how much energy the sound is produced.

Vowels are traditionally described by specifying the size and shape of the resonance chambers in the mouth and pharynx determined by the position of tongue and lips. There are three main descriptive criteria (*vowel parameters*):

- *lip position* (unrounded–rounded)
- *vertical tongue position* (high–low, or closed–open)
- *horizontal tongue position* (front–back).

In order to understand what this means in practice, we will try one experiment for each of these criteria. It is important that these should be done silently so as not to allow the sound to distract you from the perception of what goes on in your mouth.

Let us start with lip rounding, which is easiest to control and to observe.

▶ TASK 13

Silently, say the word 'tea' and then alternate it with 'two': 'tea–two–tea–two'. Concentrate your attention on how you slowly and deliberately spread the lips for articulating one, and how you round them for the other.

The second criterion for describing vowels is the distance between the roof of the mouth and the surface of the tongue, which determines the size of the oral resonance chamber and thus vowel quality. This is usually called tongue height, or degree of opening/closing. It parallels the length of the column of air vibrating in the resonance chamber of, say, a flute: long for low tones, short for high tones.

▶ TASK 14

Silently say the following sequences of words, paying attention to the way the mouth gets progressively more open with the different vowels:

beat–bait–bet–bat

too–toe–paw–pa.

Then try the same words again, but this time bite the end of a pencil to hold your teeth about one centimetre apart (but without it interfering with movements of the tongue). Holding the jaw rigid in this manner, try to become clearly aware of the different degrees of tongue-raising.
(*adapted from Catford 1988: 126–7*)

This Task is meant to make you aware that tongue height can be varied by lowering the jaw, or by keeping the lower jaw still and progressively lowering and flattening the tongue. Usually both work together in varying vertical tongue position and thus regulating the degree of openness of vowels.

The third criterion for describing vowels is the relative advancement or retraction of the body of the tongue in the mouth, usually called horizontal tongue position. This criterion allows us to categorize vowels as 'front vowels' (such as [i]) and 'back vowels' (such as [u]).

▶ TASK 15

Repeat Task 13. This time try to keep your lips neutral and relaxed and watch your tongue moving back and forth in the mouth as you say 'tea–two–tea–two'.

This brings us to the end of our exploration of the basic parameters according to which vowels can be classified: rounded or unrounded, closed or open, front or back. These criteria constitute what is called *vowel quality*. Another descriptive feature concerns the relative length of the vowel, *vowel quantity*. These criteria together can be used, in principle, to describe all vowels of all natural languages. In order to do this, it is useful to establish in principle which vowels it is possible for humans to produce, to map out the area within which vowels can be articulated. This idea was put into practice by the eminent English phonetician Daniel Jones. He introduced a set of universal reference vowels, the so-called *Cardinal Vowels*, based on the notion of a 'vowel space' within the mouth. Beyond this 'vowel limit' vowels cannot be articulated. For instance, the Cardinal Vowel [i] is the highest possible vowel, produced nearest the front of the mouth.

▶ **TASK 16**

> Silently first, produce a prolonged English /i:/ as in 'see' and hold it for a while. Notice how your tongue is bunched up high in the front of your mouth, and feel the airstream escaping through a narrow channel between your tongue and the hard palate. Now voice this i-sound and pronounce a prolonged [iiiiiiiiii]. While you do this, make your tongue very tense and gradually push it further towards the hard palate, until you can hear some friction. This is the point where the vowel stops being a vowel and turns into a consonant, namely a fricative.

This Task helped us explore what is meant by 'vowel limit' and 'vowel space'.

The purpose of the Cardinal Vowels is to enable us to specify virtually any vowel of any language with reference to them. This principle was adopted by the International Phonetic Association (*IPA*), which established a general framework for the description (and transcription) of both vowels and consonants for all languages with reference to the criteria of classification we have already discussed.

It is important to emphasize that articulation needs to be experienced to be understood, and that this understanding should lead to an awareness of how sounds are actually produced, not simply a technical vocabulary for describing them. There is no point in teachers just telling their students that the consonant in the English word 'fee' is a 'voiceless labio-dental fricative'.

2.2 Sounds in the mind

Acoustic facts are around us all the time. We are usually able to recognize sounds (music, a door shutting, the sound of typing, etc.), but occasionally we are at a loss and our reaction is 'What's that noise?' The reason for this is simply that in such cases we have no previous experience of the sound which would allow us to ascribe it a cause, let alone invest it with meaning.

It would seem that humans have a mental 'filter' phasing out noise which is irrelevant so that we become fully aware of noise only when it becomes obtrusive, or if we have to concentrate very hard, as is the case, for instance, when we are listening to an unfamiliar foreign language.

Our perception is also influenced by another, more permanent, kind of filter, that concerning our knowledge of the sound system as a code. Native listeners have a predisposition for regarding certain kinds of acoustic information as significant and others as not. The kind of information we regard as significant depends on what we have come to regard as such during first language acquisition, for at that stage we learnt to segment the acoustic chaos around us into significant units. What we are not aware of is the fact that they are significant by convention only, and that other conventions are possible. Usually this is first brought home to us when we struggle with some of the sounds of a foreign language. It is important to realize, however, that this conventional first language filter is likely to remain in operation when we are exposed to a second or any other language. As long as our first language filter is 'on' we cannot even perceive differences which are crucial in the second language. We can only participate in what is new with reference to what is familiar.

But as teachers we need to be able to assume a different stance, that of analyst, to offset the tendency to see other languages in terms of our own. In order to be able to explain certain aspects of pronunciation, we require a framework which allows us to describe the systematic sound pattern of the (foreign) language we teach and, ideally, to contrast it with our students' first language(s).

So how do we talk about the speech sounds we produce, and how do we compare the speech sounds of different languages? Not only do we need a knowledge of how these sounds are produced as physiological and acoustic events (the domain of *phonetics*), but also an understanding of how they are utilized, how they are organized into a system of sounds in the language concerned (the domain of *phonology*).

▶   TASK 17

This is a kind of puzzle. Consider the transcription of the word 'lock' /lɒk/. By replacing only one sound at a time, we can make up a 'chain' of new words: /lɒk/–/lɪk/–/lɪt/–/sɪt/ (now all three sounds are different from the initial word), and then work our way 'backwards' to complete the circle: /sɪt/–/sɪk/–/sɒk/–/lɒk/. Now try the same with the words 'pat' /pæt/ and 'meal' /miːl/. You may find you need to write the words down.

The sounds which were exchanged to make up new words are distinctive sounds of English, because they distinguish one word from another. Thus what distinguishes 'lock' from 'lick' is the contrast between the vowels /ɒ/ and /ɪ/, while 'lick' and 'tick' are different words solely because of the contrast between the consonants /l/ and /t/. The term for such word pairs which differ only in one sound is *minimal pairs*. The contrastive, or distinctive, sounds of a language are called *phonemes*.

▶ # TASK 18

Consider the short vowels in a language other than English. Can you think of a minimal pair based on the contrast between a sound like /ɒ/ as in 'lock' and a sound like /ɪ/ as in 'lick'? Next, can you produce a minimal pair based on the contrast between /æ/ as in 'pat' and /e/ as in 'pet'?

Most languages have o-like, i-like, and e-like phonemes; many languages, however, do not have a phoneme like English /æ/. It is therefore very likely that you could think of a minimal pair of the 'lock–lick' type, but you should not be surprised if you could not come up with a pair of the 'pat–pet' kind. This illustrates the fact that languages select different parts of the sound spectrum (vowels and consonants) for linguistic use. The Cardinal Vowel concept introduced in **2.1** can help us explore this difference with reference to vowels. Different languages divide the vowel space differently. As Catford (1988: 189 ff.) has pointed out, the [i]–[ɑ] continuum is segmented differently in English and Spanish. In English we have six segments: /iː/ as in 'leek', /ɪ/ as in 'lick', the diphthong /eɪ/ as in 'late', /e/ as in 'let', /æ/ as in 'latter', and /ɑː/ as in 'lark'. In contrast with these six vowel sounds, in Spanish we have only three: /i/ as in 'ibis', /e/ as in 'eres', and /a/ as in 'acá' (examples from Catford). This is not to say that Spanish speakers cannot produce [iː] or [æ], they just do not use these sounds systematically for the creation of meaning.

Languages very 'remote' from English often treat sounds as distinctive which English speakers did not even know existed. Examples are clicks in certain African languages, and pharyngeal and glottal sounds in Arabic. The use of pitch to express lexical or grammatical contrasts (for example, tense) is another possibility not exploited in English and most other Indo-European languages. But the majority of the world's languages are actually tone languages, and have distinctive pitch levels which are like distinctive sounds, or phonemes, in that the meaning of a word depends on the pitch level at which it is spoken. Echoing the term *phoneme*, we call these distinctive pitch levels *tonemes*. The example quoted in practically every introduction to the subject (so why not here?) is Mandarin Chinese /mɑ/, which represents four different words, depending on the associated tone:

ma[1] (with high level pitch)   'mother'

ma[2] (with high rising pitch)   'hemp' (a plant)

ma[3] (with low, or falling then rising pitch) 'horse'

ma[4] (with falling pitch)   'scold'
(Clark and Yallop 1990: 286)

But even in related languages there can be sounds with features which are difficult for foreign learners: think of the proverbial problems English speakers have with the nasalized French vowels (as in *demain, non*), or with German [x] (as in *lachen*) and [ø:] (as in *schön*).

Describing and comparing sounds
The notion of phonemes enables us to describe the speech sounds of particular languages systematically. Whenever we talk about systems (not just of sounds but of anything at all), the notion of opposition is a crucial one: two elements in a system are constitutive components of that system only if they stand in opposition to one another. Thus in the realm of grammar, for instance, we refer to oppositions such as singular–plural, present tense–past tense, and statement–question (see Batstone 1994, *Grammar*, published in this series). What is important to note, however, is that although we talk about oppositions, or systematic differences, we can only do so if there is also something these elements have in common, if we know with reference to which criterion element A and element B are different. For example, singular and plural are oppositions with regard to grammatical number. Similarly, there are criteria by which differences between phonemes are described. As was indicated on pages 14–17, these are quality and quantity for vowels, and place, manner, and force of articulation for consonants.

▶ **TASK 19**

Refer to **2.1**.

Decide which criteria you would use to describe the initial consonants in 'king' and 'thing'. In which way(s) are they similar, in which are they different?

Decide which criteria you would use to describe the difference between the vowels in 'net' and 'nought'.

The consonants /θ/ and /k/ are different on two of the three dimensions. Both are fortis (voiceless) consonants, but they differ in manner of articulation: /θ/ is a fricative, and /k/ is a plosive. They are also articulated in a different place: /k/ at the very back of the mouth (velar) and /θ/ with the tip of the tongue against the upper teeth (dental). The two vowels are different in length (quantity) and horizontal tongue position: the vowel in 'net' is short and front, while the vowel in 'nought' is long and back. The vertical tongue position is roughly the same, namely neither open nor closed.

It is obvious that mapping out the 'territory' of the phonemic systems of specific languages can help us identify 'gaps' in one language where another language may have significant speech sounds. This enables us to compare and contrast phonemes, and entire phoneme inventories, across languages with reference to fairly clearly defined criteria. For instance, we can say that French has a rounded front vowel /y/ (as in *buffet*) which does not exist in English, or that English has two dental fricatives, lenis /ð/ and fortis /θ/, which many other languages do not have. This comparison across languages, or contrastive analysis, is often used as a starting point for developing syllabuses for pronunciation teaching.

Phonemes and allophones

What is not represented by the phoneme system is the actual phonetic realization of these distinctive sounds. No two realizations of a phoneme, even by the same person, are ever exactly the same. In addition, there are individual and dialectal differences between the accents of different speakers even though they may all consider themselves to be speaking the same language, with the same phoneme inventory. In other words, phonemic value and phonetic realizations are two different things. What we may think of as 'the same sound' may not actually be pronounced in the same way.

▶ ## TASK 20

> This is another silent experiment. Without uttering a sound, get ready to pronounce the words 'geese' and 'goose'. Observe the position and shape of your tongue and lips: how do they differ in preparation for saying the two words?
> *(adapted from Kreidler 1989: 9)*

You will have observed that for both words, the back of your tongue is raised, touching the roof of the mouth towards the back. But while your lips are spread for 'geese', they are rounded for 'goose'. Now, if you were asked whether 'geese' and 'goose' start with the same sound, your answer would probably be: yes, with /g/. The point is, however, that they start with the same phoneme, but that the phoneme is pronounced slightly differently in the company of different sounds, that is to say in different environments. The different realizations of phonemes in speech are called *allophones*.

The fact that we perceive the two allophones of /g/ as 'the same' is due to the fact that we idealize when we process speech. Idealization is a useful and necessary strategy common to all systematic enquiry. It enables us to reduce the complexity of 'linguistic reality' in order to account for it by organizing it into categories. The categories we are concerned with here are phonemic ones.

We might consider some more examples. We said that in RP there is a long i-sound, /iː/, as in 'see' /siː/, and a short i-sound, /ɪ/, as in sit /sɪt/. But what about the pair 'seat'–'sieve'? *Phonemically* speaking, in abstract categories, we also have a long /iː/ in 'seat' and a short /ɪ/ in 'sieve'. *Phonetically*, however, that is, in actual realization, the i-sound in 'sieve' may well be just as long as that in 'seat', due to the shortening effect of the final plosive. This is also the reason why some linguists object to the long–short distinction and prefer the terms *tense* (for /iː/) and *lax* (for /ɪ/), according to the degree of muscle tension required to produce the respective vowels.

▶ **TASK 21**

Pronounce the word 'lull' /lʌl/. Is there a difference between the two actualizations of the phoneme /l/? If yes, how would you describe it? In the same vein, pronounce the word pair 'pin'–'spin'. What difference do you notice between the realizations of the p-phoneme?

These examples demonstrate two more ways in which the environment of sounds may influence their realizations. The l-sound in RP is 'clear', or 'light', when followed by a vowel, but 'dark' when followed by a consonant or a pause. In the case of 'pin'–'spin', it is the /s/ which makes all the difference: while /p/ (and the other fortis plosives /t/ and /k/) are normally *aspirated* (i.e. said with a little puff of air) when in initial position in a stressed syllable, they are not aspirated when preceded by /s/.

▶ **TASK 22**

Japanese learners of English tend to have problems with the distinction between /l/ and /r/. For instance, one of the present authors was recently asked by a Japanese professor of English, 'Do you say /lɪˈspekt/ or /rɪˈspekt/?' (for 'respect'). How do you explain the difficulty this learner has?

The above example shows us that while /l/ and /r/ are two distinct phonemes in English, they are only perceived as allophones in Japanese.

The differences we have been exploring here are those between phonemic, or 'emic' categories on the one hand and phonetic, or 'etic' ones on the other. 'Emic', then, refers to features of the system, whereas 'etic' denotes features of actual realizations. Another pair of terms expressing the same idea is *phoneme* as abstract phonological entity and *allophone* as phonetic behavioural event. We could thus say that clear [l] and dark [ɫ] are allophones of the phoneme /l/. Note that the convention is to use slashes / / for phonemes and square brackets [ ] for allophones.

It should be clear from the discussion in this unit that we 'think in phonemes' but that we 'speak in allophones'. The reason for this is that we do not articulate sounds in isolation, but connect them up in strings. In 3 we will look at connected speech in more detail.

3 Connected speech

The following illustration shows the vibrations of the vocal cords during the phrase 'apples, lemons, and cherries' spoken by an American from California.

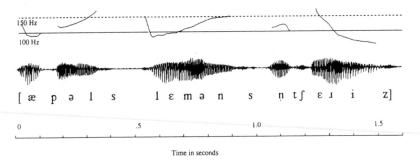

(Ladefoged 1993: 185)

Oscillograms like this can clarify one very important point: speech is a continuum without clear-cut borderlines between individual sounds. Thus, in natural conversation, if somebody asks us the question 'Where are your jeans?', we are most likely to hear something like [weəjɔːdʒiːnz]—and may even perceive it as 'Wear yuh jeans'.

3.1 Stringing sounds together

We said in 2 that to speak about 'the articulation of phoneme x in language y' is to simplify something that is in fact much more intricate. At the production stage, speech is not an assembly of distinct articulatory movements, each of which corresponds to one phoneme. Our speech is a continuous stream of transitions and approximations in which the 'ideal' positions for the articulation of individual sounds may never be reached.

We can draw an analogy with handwriting here: the handwriting of most adults is only an approximation of the models presented for imitation at primary school.

▶ **TASK 23**

Are some of *your* handwriting styles more faithful to such a model than others? Compare a note written to yourself to one written for pinning up on the staff room notice board.

The analogy between speech and handwriting suggested here is quite far-reaching. Individuals differ in the degree to which their handwriting strays from an idealized model. In both speech and handwriting, time pressure is an important factor leading to short cuts and simplifications. In both speech and writing we are quite happy with the distorted acoustic and graphic shapes produced by people we are familiar with, but we tend to be more explicit if we produce language for strangers. Thus, in spoken discourse, speakers adapt their production to their audience and articulate with maximal efficiency rather than maximal clarity. The important thing is to get the message across.

In order to recognize distorted shapes as versions of some ideal model, we need to have a mental image of the model. The creation of this mental image is enacted by visible physical movements when we learn to write. But how do we achieve it for the spoken language? Research has shown that maternal speech to children at very early stages is in many ways phonologically clarified in order to provide idealized input. We could say that babies are exposed to a kind of foreigner-talk. In addition, however, mothers alternate between clarified and 'distorted' forms and this seems to enable the children to develop rules of correspondence between the model and the distorted forms they will normally encounter (Ratner 1984).

On our way to becoming competent speakers, we thus acquire an idealized mental image of a word in terms of all the sounds it is made up of. Later, we need the full information only if a word occurs in isolation, because in this case we need to identify it by the acoustic information alone. Usually, however, the acoustic information is supported by our knowledge on various other levels.

▶ **TASK 24**

Have you ever listened to a synthetic voice giving information (for example, announcing the time over the telephone)? What is your reaction to such a voice?

Maybe you get impatient because you have to listen to things you do not want to know until the required information comes along; maybe you even get annoyed because this over-explicitness is delivered in a painstakingly precise version of every sound. With human speakers, articulatory (over)-precision is a stylistic device. It is a conscious choice if we want to be insistent or threatening, but it may also make us sound 'wearyingly precise and pedantic, even offensively so' (Brown 1990: 130)—which may be exactly how we perceive synthetic voices. In human interaction, articulatory imprecision is clearly the more natural and the more functional option.

As native listeners we seem to make up for this imprecision effortlessly by deftly integrating an immense amount of support knowledge in order to make sense of the messages we get. In real-life interaction, phonetically ambiguous pairs like 'I scream'/'ice cream' are hardly ever a problem because we are actively making predictions about what syntactic forms and lexical items are likely to occur in a given context or situation (see Anderson and Lynch 1988, *Listening* in this series).

▶ TASK 25

Austin and Carter (1988: 21–2) tell the following anecdote:

'Late one Friday afternoon a colleague came into our research laboratory, and a listener heard "Next Thursday at night, you're invited to a party for (. . .). We're going to the Peking restaurant and have lunch." The listener replied, "Have lunch at night?" The colleague said, "No, lunch, at lunch, on the ninth." The listener said, "Are you sure you said the ninth?" '

Can you find an explanation for this misperception?

As in the 'jeans' example above, the acoustic signal between 'night' and 'ninth' may have been indistinct, and the hearer perceived what seemed most likely from the immediate context, 'party', namely 'night'. Moreover, he perhaps did not expect to hear the day of the week plus the date in an informal announcement. On hearing the word 'lunch', however, his interpretation is disconfirmed so he stops the conversation to ask for clarification.

As native listeners we hear what seems most plausible to us in a given context. Moreover, we prefer to hear words which are frequent and therefore familiar to us. In other words, we use top-down processing. Just how much implicit knowledge feeds into our communication with others often becomes evident as soon as we enter a different dialect area of our native language. The situation is much more taxing, of course, when we are trying to understand a foreign language. Brown says about non-native speakers that:

'For complex social and psychological reasons they are less sure that they have grasped the topic being spoken of, the opinion being expressed about it, and the reasons for the speaker wanting to talk about it. They are less sure of the relevance of their own past experience in helping them to arrive at an interpretation'.
(Brown 1990: 59–60)

▶   TASK 26

Eavesdropping on conversations on buses and trains is a good example. Have you ever been frustrated and plagued with doubts about your competence in your own language when you did not understand a conversation going on in the seat behind you? How about the same situation in a foreign country where you knew some of the language? What did you feel you needed to know?

Non-native speakers are often insecure in their judgements about the plausibility and relevance of the forms they are hearing. There is also a second kind of contextual information which feeds into the understanding of speech: our expectations about the frequency of lexical items and the statistical probabilities of one form co-occurring with certain others. Second language learners have often not been able to develop intuitions and expectations about word frequencies, the likelihood that a word will occur in a particular situation, or even what counts as a 'standard situation'. Non-native speakers make up for their lack of competence in these two respects by being more analytical. They rely—often exclusively—on acoustic information alone. Things are even worse for learners who have been taught with heavy emphasis on correctness and precision. They suffer a 'devastating diminution of phonetic information at the segmental level when they encounter normal speech' (Brown 1990: 60). In **3.2** we shall look at a number of processes at the sound level which cause this devastating effect, and what could be done about teaching them.

3.2 Sound simplifications

We have seen that in connected speech, our aim is usually not maximal distinctiveness but maximal ease of communication. As speakers, we therefore tend to minimize articulatory effort and maximize ease of articulation, because we can rely on the fact that our listeners will be using different types of knowledge in understanding our message. In minimizing our efforts in articulation, we tend to make adjacent sounds more like each other (*assimilation*), and sometimes we leave a sound out altogether (*elision*), but we may also insert a sound in order to make for a smoother transition (*linking*). All this happens within words, but when words are combined in the stream of speech their edges also become available for this. It is noticeable, though, that it is above all the ends of words which are affected. The beginnings of words are too important for identification. And although the tendency towards simplification and ease of articulation is universal, different languages and different dialects of the same language may follow different paths. Therefore, when we now go on to look more closely at the main simplification strategies, much of what is said about English will hold true for other languages too, but not all.

Adjustment to surroundings: assimilation

If we look at each speech sound as a set of movements, it is only natural that series of movements as they occur in connected speech will influence each other. When we speak at normal speed, individual sound segments follow each other so quickly that the tongue may never reach the 'ideal position' connected with a particular sound. It will only approximate to this position before it moves on to the position necessary for the next segment. The exact position of the tongue and other articulators during a segment therefore depends on where the tongue is coming from and where it is going to: it depends on the neighbouring sounds. This is the main reason, as we have seen, why phonemes have a variety of different realizations (allophones). Thus, in all languages which allow a sequence /ki/, the allophone of /k/ which occurs in the neighbourhood of /i/ will be pronounced further forward on the palate than the allophone of /k/ which occurs before /əu/, as in 'kiss' vs. 'cope'. Exactly how far forward or back the /k/ moves will depend on the individual language (compare Task 20).

While, theoretically, any sound may influence any other, in practice assimilation is restricted to a limited subset of a language's phonemes. In English, these sounds are mainly /t/, /d/, and /h/ when followed by a syllable/word-initial velar or labial consonant /k/, /g/, /m/, or /b/.

▶ # TASK 27

Here are some examples. The first (phonetic) transcription renders colloquial speech, while the second (phonemic) transcription represents the 'ideal' shape of the word(s). The symbol [ʔ] represents the *glottal stop*.

apartment	[əˈpɑːʔpmənt]	/əˈpɑːtmənt/
Great Britain	[ɡreɪʔpˈbrɪtn]	/ɡreɪtˈbrɪtən/
won't come	[wəʊnʔˈkʌm]	/wəʊntˈkʌm/
banned for life	[ˌbæmbfəˈlaɪf]	/ˌbændfəˈlaɪf/
down by law	[ˌdaʊmbaɪˈlɔː]	/ˌdaʊnbaɪˈlɔː/
pancake	[ˈpæŋkeɪk]	/ˈpænkeɪk/

Find some more instances of assimilations across word-boundaries and try to transcribe them.

When looking for further examples, you might have noticed that English past tense forms including participles (such as 'listened to', 'reduced control', 'a recognized treatment') provide a great number of assimilations of the sounds /d/ and /t/. These two sounds will also figure prominently in the next simplification process.

Elision

When we minimize our effort, the articulation of sounds is weakened: perhaps we do not close our lips fully for a /p/, or the friction of a /ð/ may almost disappear. If the articulation is weakened too much, the sound may disappear altogether. This second very common simplification process is called elision: a consonant or a vowel which would be present in a carefully pronounced version of the word or phrase is left out.

Naturally, it is the vowels from unstressed syllables which are the first to go in not-so-careful pronunciation: the *schwa* in many final unstressed syllables disappears. Compare the careful pronunciation of 'practical' ['præktɪkəl] with the quick ['præktɪkl].

▶ # TASK 28

Look up how the pronunciation of the following words is indicated in a dictionary such as the *Oxford Advanced Learner's Dictionary*, and see how the unstressed vowels are treated:

natural	penitentiary
exoticism	camera

In all cases, RP allows elision of at least one schwa per word, which is probably why RP sounds 'clipped' to speakers of varieties which do not follow this trend to such an extent (for example, American English).

As for consonants, it is /t/ and /d/ which are most commonly involved in elision. When there is a sequence of three consonants, it is nearly always a /t/ or a /d/ which ends up in the middle, both inside words ('Christmas') and across word boundaries ('must be'). Very often, /d/ also elides when it is preceded by a vowel but followed by a consonant ('there could be' as [ðə'kʊbi]).

▶ # TASK 29

Mark or transcribe the consonant sequences in the following words and phrases and look especially at the position of /t/ and /d/. Be careful not to let the spelling mislead you in some cases. How would you pronounce these words and phrases? Ask some other speakers to read them out quickly.

dialects	We distinguish between accents and dialects.
dustbin	A dustbin was hurled through the window.
hurled through the	A dustbin was hurled through the window.
and then	. . . well and then they said . . .
as confused as ever	No change, he's as confused as ever.
wanted to	I've always wanted to tell you that.
must be	This must be her!

There are clearly varying degrees to which elision is obligatory here, ranging from 'dustbin' (always elided) to 'as confused as ever' (only in fast speech).

In addition to /t/ and /d/, which are elided by all speakers, there are also some other consonants which are elided quite frequently. These include /v/ and /ð/. Here are some examples: '5 p.m.' [fai:pi:'em], 'needs of the' ['ni:dzəðə], 'went the way of the' [wentə'wei:ðə]. Note how the diphthongs in the first and third examples are transcribed as having extra length in compensation for the loss of the preposition 'of'. Brown (1990: 68ff.) discusses many more.

Linking

In discussing elision we saw that the common strategy for dealing with sequences of consonants is to elide one of them. But what happens when two vowel-sounds meet at a word boundary, as in 'How are you?'? Theoretically, we could envisage dropping one of them.

▶   ## TASK 30

Experiment with dropping one of the adjacent vowels in the phrases below:

'how often', 'we ought', 'for better or for worse', 'they are here', 'far away', 'you and me'.

It is likely that you found that except for 'you'n me' this sounded impossible because the words were distorted beyond recognition. Eliding adjacent vowels does not seem to work for English. In fact, what English speakers do in such cases is the opposite of elision: they insert an extra sound in order to mark the transition between the two vowels.

In accents of English such as RP which do not pronounce the /r/ after vowels (for example, 'port', 'car', 'better'), the 'r' which is present in the spelling is activated in such cases ('better or worse', 'far away', 'took the car and drove off'). Sometimes speakers also insert an /r/ where the orthography does not warrant it: 'That's the idea^r of it' [ðætsðɔɪjaɪ'dɪə'vɪt], for example. This has been called the *intrusive 'r'*. It is interesting to note that no speakers of the 'r-less' accents of English use the linking 'r' and the intrusive 'r' a hundred per cent of the time. Some speakers use them more often than others but all use them occasionally, even though they may say they never do, as there is a certain amount of social stigmatization connected with the use of the intrusive 'r'. Incidentally, this raises another difficulty about the model of speech behaviour to be used in the teaching of pronunciation, as discussed in **1.1.**

In other cases where there is no /r/ available, speakers use another consonantal sound which is very close to the first of the two vowels: if the first word ends in a u-type vowel a /w/ is inserted; if the first word ends in an i-type vowel a /j/ is inserted. As neither is articulated fully, they are usually rendered like this in a transcription: 'how often' [ˈhaʊʷˈɒfən], 'they are' [ˈðeɪʲˈɑː].

Another process which is connected with this is the tendency of English speakers to treat word-final consonants as if they belonged to the next word, especially if that word starts with a vowel. This obscuring of the word boundary leads to famous homophonous pairs such as 'I scream'/'ice cream', 'an aim'/'a name', 'new display'/'nudist play', or the jocular 'get up at eight o'clock'/'get a potato clock'. For experienced speakers with plenty of supplementary knowledge these are hardly ever a problem, as they normally occur in a context which excludes one of the pair. Inexperienced learners, however, may have severe difficulties in deciding where the word boundary lies: is the sequence [keɪmɪn] to be analysed as [ˈkeɪ ˈmɪn] 'Kay Min' or [keɪm ˈɪn] 'came in'?

▶ # TASK 31

Redraw the word-boundaries in the following examples by treating the final consonant of the first word as if it belonged to the second word. In which cases is the second 'word' a possible word of the English language?

Example: came in [keɪ mɪn]: 'min' = not a possible word

dish out, rage on, laugh about, grab it, march in, carves up, not at all, an(d) out, an old dog.

An inexperienced learner may thus hear 'shout', 'John', 'bit', 'chin', or 'tall', but also [fəbaʊt], [tə], [naʊt], [sʌp], and [nəʊld], and will be left wondering what these words mean or how they can be made to fit the context of the conversation. ('Sup' and 'nowt' are English words, but their currency is restricted.)

We have seen how the connected speech processes of assimilation, elision, and linking alter the appearance of words, making them differ from the ideal shape which they have when pronounced in isolation. It is likely that the experience common to all listeners to a foreign language, namely that the natives 'speak very fast', is due to this lack of phonetic information about words and their boundaries.

4   Stress

4.1 The nature of stress

In English, we can use the word 'stress' to refer generally to the way we emphasize something or give it prominence. So we talk about stressing (or putting particular stress on) a point: 'I would like to stress that ...'. Here, obviously, we are referring to language at the level of discourse. But we also use the term to refer more specifically to the sounds of speech. If we listen to spoken language we can hear that certain elements seem to be given more prominence or emphasis.

▶   TASK 32

In your own language, what tells you that a word is stressed?

Write your answer down.

Try to get hold of a stretch of speech from a language you do not know at all and listen for the stresses.

Maybe you found that it was quite hard to pick out what was stressed and what was not, even though you were quite sure from your own language that the stresses seemed distinctly louder than the rest. Apparently it is our knowledge of the language system that makes us pick out certain cues from the soundstream and ascribe to them the value 'stress'.

Before looking more closely at what these cues are, we need to be quite clear that the term *stress* is used in two different ways. One use is as a conventional label for the overall prominence of certain syllables over others. Used in this wider sense, stress does not correlate directly and simply with one feature such as loudness, but represents the combined effect of several other factors besides. It is in this general sense that we can say that Finnish words are stressed on the first syllable, Polish words are stressed on the last but one, or that the English words 'father' and 'lengthen' are stressed on the first syllable.

The second, and narrower, use of the term stress is concerned with the way in which speakers actually achieve this impression of prominence, i.e. its physiological cause. In this narrower sense, stress refers to the muscular energy which goes into the production of a syllable.

Few authors are as clear as Catford in their distinction between stress as 'linguistic foregrounding function' and stress as 'muscular effort in production', even though the two clearly belong to different levels of analysis. The first definition is the one most commonly used in pronunciation textbooks. We will first review in some more detail how stress (muscular energy) contributes to stress (prominence). After this we will be dealing exclusively with stress as prominence.

We can look at stress as muscular energy from two points of view: that of the physiological activity of the speaker, and that of the perceptual activity of the listener.

The production of stress

In producing the continuous soundstream of speech, speakers do not keep up a steady degree of articulatory energy: over some stretches the energy level in the articulatory and respiratory muscles is higher than in others.

▶ ## TASK 33

Take a good breath and say a long, drawn-out [s]. Now deliberately vary the amount of air you use in producing this voiceless fricative sound. Drive out the air in an alternating series of stronger and weaker bursts [sSsS]; you can vary the pattern [SSsSSs], etc.

(adapted from Catford 1988: 173)

You probably noticed that 'something happened' in your rib-cage; if you have a very mobile diaphragm, you may have consciously used it to increase the pressure on your lungs to drive out more air. You may also have noticed that once you started alternating the force on the [s] it stopped being one drawn-out [s] and turned into several successive 's's, i.e. syllables consisting of an [s]. It is important to keep in mind that stress does not just affect sounds but whole syllables.

There is a natural physical connection between stress and pitch, as the stronger airstream automatically increases the number of vibrations of the vocal cords, causing a rise in pitch. Pitch can be neutralized if we 'switch off' the vocal cords in a whisper. But speakers do not usually whisper, and therefore the presence of stress is often concealed by, and confused with, its accompanying pitch change. The connection between stress and duration should perhaps be formulated in less general terms: in many languages, among them English, greater articulatory energy is accompanied by a longer duration of the affected syllable. In its function of indicating prominence, stress thus seems to be a combination of the factors energy, pitch, and duration.

The perception of stress
In answer to the question 'What is stress?' many people would probably spontaneously mention 'loudness' as the key to their perception of stress. Somehow, stressed syllables seem to be louder than the rest.

▶ ## TASK 34

Repeat Task 33 with the sounds [sSsS], [fFfFf], and [ʃʃʃʃ]. Compare the loudness of a stressed 'f' with that of an unstressed 'sh'. What is your impression?

Differences in inherent loudness can also be found with vowel sounds: you may have to stress an isolated [i] quite strongly to make it sound as loud as a rather weakly stressed [a]. It thus turns out that absolute loudness is not very helpful in explaining our perception of stress. This does not, however, mean that 'loudness' cannot be a valid impressionistic term. The intuitive appeal of the term 'loudness' may have to do with the fact that we subconsciously correlate the sounds we hear with the energy that went into their production and call it loudness. What we should be careful about is relying exclusively on loudness in the teaching of stress in a particular language.

What, then, are the decisive cues we should look for in the perception of stress? As far as English is concerned, according to Fry (1958) it is pitch changes which are the most reliable cues in the perception of stress, followed by duration. Experiments with speakers of other languages have corroborated the importance of pitch as a cue in the perception of stress, but they have also shown that the relative weight of the factors involved is definitely language specific. In English, for instance, the duration of syllables seems to be a more important cue than in other languages.

4.2 The syllable

We have repeatedly mentioned the term *syllable*, but without defining it. The fact that this was possible without (hopefully) causing too much confusion is symptomatic: everybody seems to have an intuitive sense of what it is. Everybody, however, finds it notoriously difficult to define it exactly. We shall look at some evidence suggesting that syllables are 'real' and then go on to review some of the definitions which have been proposed. We shall see that these definitions depend very much on our view of what the syllable 'does' in language, and we will therefore have to touch upon the most important functions of the syllable-unit in language processing.

▶ TASK 35

The following words were taken at random from (every 100th page of) the *Oxford Advanced Learner's Dictionary*:

abundance, biennial, clarify, deaden, equanimity, gag, lavish, province, ruefulness, smilingly, synthetically.

How many syllables does each word have? Ask several other speakers of English. Alternatively, if there are not many English speakers at hand, do the same with a similarly random word-list from your own language.

You probably found this easy and so did the persons you asked. There may be some contested cases, but on the whole speakers of English agree about the number of syllables in words.

The relevance of the syllable as a language-unit seems to be borne out by the history of writing: syllabaries are, after all, older than alphabets. For those of us who are familiar only with an alphabetic writing system, the existence of single letters suggests that speech is segmented into individual sounds. However, people who have not been taught an alphabetic writing system find it easy to syllabify words but difficult to segment them into sounds. This also holds true for pre-school children, who have *not yet* been taught an alphabetic writing system.

Slips of the tongue provide further evidence for the 'reality' of syllables. Sound substitutions do not occur randomly, but follow a definite pattern. Most frequently the beginnings of syllables are exchanged: 'par cark' for 'car park', 'e-fə-lənt' for 'e-lə-fənt', and so on.

So far we have simply looked at evidence suggesting that the syllable really does exist. But how can we define it? There are two groups of definitions, none of which is entirely satisfactory: one focusing on the physical, the other on the mental side of things.

The classical physical definition of the syllable says that syllables come about because the air leaves our lungs in little puffs rather than a continuous stream. This is also known as the 'chest-pulse-theory' of the syllable and it explains why the syllable is intuitively sensed by speakers of all languages. However, not everyone locates syllable boundaries at the same place.

▶ TASK 36

Take the word 'Atlantic' /ətlæntɪk/. There are clearly three syllables centring around the vowels /ə–æ–ɪ/. But there is more than one way of dividing up the consonants in between. One way is 'at-lan-tic'. How many other ways of syllabifying this word can you find? Do all these syllable divisions work equally well for English? Do they work for some other language you know?

You probably found that the syllabifications which counted /tl/ into one syllable (a-tlan-tic, atl-an-tic) or which made /nt/ the beginning of a syllable (a-tla-ntic) were somehow 'not English' but might well be normal in some other language. Decisions about how to break a word into syllables are clearly language dependent. The only truly general statement we can make is that every syllable has a peak, i.e. the vowels in Task 36 above. Apart from that, every language has its own rules determining what sounds can appear before and after the peak and in which combinations. The most widespread syllable type seems to be the one consisting of one consonant (C) plus one vowel (V), i.e. CV. Some languages, such as Japanese, do not allow syllables to be more complex than this.

▶ ## TASK 37

What syllable types do the following English words represent?

Example: 'flip' /flɪp/ CCVC

            'scraped' /skreɪpt/ CCCVCC

awe	cat	saw	elk	flee
eat	stop	springs	strict	

Are there any restrictions as to the actual combinations of consonants? For instance, try to think of other words with three consonants at the beginning. What is the first consonant in each case?

Task 37 is straightforward: 'awe' is a V-syllable, 'cat' CVC, 'saw' CV, 'elk' VCC, 'flee' CCV, 'eat' VC, 'stop' CCVC, 'springs' CCCVCC, and 'strict' CCCVCC. In English, if a syllable has three initial consonants, the first one is always /s/; a syllable may end with the sequence /nd/ ('end') but it cannot start with /nd/ (*'ndoll'). There is a fairly large number of such combinatory restrictions (Kreidler 1989: 117–38). In Spanish, for instance, a word-initial syllable may never start with the sequences /sp/, /st/, or /sk/. That is why 'Spain' is *España* and the Latin word *stella* ('star') became *estrella*. In Japanese, on the other hand, as we have seen, syllables may only have a single consonant initially and no consonant at all in syllable-final position. Thus, if Japanese rules were to operate on the English one-syllable word /stiks/, they would break up the *consonant clusters* and each consonant would have to be regarded as a syllable in its own right: something like sə-ti-kə-sə would emerge as a consequence.

Thus, while the concept of the syllable itself is universal, the exact shape of what a syllable should, or indeed can, look like is not. We acquire this 'feeling' for the shape of a 'proper syllable' when we learn our native language. That this is a long-term process becomes obvious when we listen to small children. We said above that the most widespread syllable-type is CV, and since this seems to be the easiest and most 'natural' option, children modify the target forms of their first language accordingly: consonant clusters are often reduced ('blue'>'bue') or final consonants deleted ('big'>'bi'). We can observe second language learners using the same strategies. Additionally, second language learners may also insert extra vowels ('tree'>'təree', 'big'>'bigə', etc). But not all second language learners use vowel insertion—exactly how they treat target-language syllables seems to be strongly dependent on their native language background (Tarone 1980; Sato 1987). Beginners, in particular, tend to treat target-language forms as if they belonged to their own language. Thus, our sense of syllable structure would seem to be part of the first-language filter we referred to in **2.2**. Thus, if the syllable structure of the second-language word is not 'legal' in the learner's own language, the sound pattern of the word is changed until it is. Let us take Egyptian Arabic as an example: in that language, /fl/ and /pl/ sequences are not 'legal', so that learners render the English words 'floor' and 'plastic' as /filɔːr/ and /bilæstik/ (Broselow 1983).

▶ **TASK 38**

Can you think of some words borrowed into English from other languages, or English pronunciations of foreign names, where adaptations of syllable structure have occurred? (For example, 'Nkomo', or 'tsetse'.)

Up to now we have mostly used one-syllable words as examples in our discussion. A problem many language users have, however, is how to divide up long, polysyllabic words. This task gets even more difficult if one looks at a second language through the 'filter' of a first language: a whole new set of choices for drawing boundaries may be available.

Further complications arise when we consider that words, mono- or polysyllabic, do not normally occur in isolation but are embedded into a stream of speech sounds. Any second language learner will confirm that in trying to understand connected speech, working out where syllables begin and end in words is the crucial problem. The difficulty of the non-native listener is due to the fact that the conditions under which rapid speech is produced affect the syllable structure of an utterance. In **3.2** we mentioned that English speakers can insert /j/ or /w/ if two vowels meet at a word-boundary. Inserting a /w/ between the /aʊ/ and the /ɒ/ in 'how often' converts a CVVCVC sequence into CVCVCVC. This may have to do with the fact that the CV syllable is the universally preferred syllable type. What it certainly does is to obscure the boundary between the words involved.

▶ TASK 39

Pretend you are shouting the word 'extraordinary' over a very bad telephone line. How many syllables do you pronounce?

Now pretend you are using the word in a quick chat with a friend. How many syllables does it have now?

Thus the number of syllables you realize may vary between six /ɪk-strə-ɔ:-dɪ-nə-ri/ and three /strɔ:-dn-ri/, depending on the situational context in which the word is pronounced. The characters in *Winnie the Pooh* pronounce this word as 'stornry', that is, even the /d/ disappears.

4.3 Word-stress

The smallest domain in which the contrast between stressed and unstressed syllables surfaces is the word. The characteristic patterning of these two kinds of syllables is commonly called *word-stress*. In some languages, describing word-stress is a simple affair: there is one general phonological rule. For instance, in Finnish and Czech it is always the first syllable in a word which receives the main stress, while in Polish it is the last but one. In the case of Spanish the rule is somewhat more detailed but still very general: stress the penultimate syllable if the word ends in a vowel, /-n/, or /-s/; otherwise stress the last syllable. In such a case we can assign word-stress, even if we do not know what the words mean.

▶ TASK 40

Considering the rules given above, mark the stressed syllables in the following words from the languages Finnish, Polish, and Spanish.

Finnish   Suomalainen, kahdeksan, kymmenen, postipankki
Polish   południe, jesień, przemysł, szczęśliwy, wymowa
Spanish congreso, ciudad, taxis, correr, alfalfa, nivel

For the assignment of word-stress in some languages, we need to know which part of the word is a suffix or a prefix, and what is the stem. Germanic stress would be such an example. Stress is normally on the stem of a word. In practice this often means that the first syllable of a word is stressed, but prefixes can of course alter this: for example, German ENde (noun: 'end') vs. beENden (verb: 'to end'), where the verb receives stress on the second syllable. Word-stress may also be sensitive to information about word-class membership: in English, for instance, two-syllable words are nearly always stressed on the first syllable if they are nouns (MOther, Attic, REcord), but if they are verbs, they are much more likely to be stressed on the second syllable (aLLOW, reCORD).

What makes English word-stress particularly difficult to cope with for foreign learners is the fact that *all* the above-mentioned factors come into play in different degrees in different parts of the vocabulary. This is what makes English word-stress appear chaotic and 'without rules'.

From the point of view of speakers of a language like Finnish or Polish, the main stress can fall almost anywhere in an English word. In this sense, English word-stress appears to be 'free'. On the other hand, we can group English words together according to where their main word-stress falls.

▶   **TASK 41**

Add a few more examples to each group:

stress on 1st syllable: enter, father, ...

stress on 2nd syllable: advice, report, ...

stress on 3rd syllable: entertain, photographic, ...

stress on 4th syllable: disinformation, variability, ...

Could we establish the above groups if English word-stress was totally free? In what sense is English word-stress fixed?

English word-stress is fixed in the sense that every word has its 'own' stress pattern which is an important part of its identity (together with its characteristic sounds and its meaning). Note that very general stress rules (as in Finnish) do not have this identity-creating effect because every word in the language has the same stress pattern.

Word-stress is also a factor of intelligibility, and is therefore relevant to the issues discussed in **1.2**. Recent models of how speakers of English recognize words in continuous speech suggest that the recognition process does not simply work sequentially, from 'left to right', one word at a time (Grosjean and Gee 1987). Rather, there is evidence that during the mental search process, the stressed syllable is picked out of the speech stream and is used to search the mental lexicon. Feasible candidates are selected from the mental lexicon on the basis of this syllable, and are then judged by how well they fit with the unstressed syllables that appear to their left and right. If this kind of model is correct, the logical consequence is that processing time and processing difficulty increase considerably if a stress appears in the wrong place. Put differently, incorrect word-stress decreases intelligibility—and may even lead to embarrassing misunderstandings.

4.4 Stress and rhythm

We have discussed the phenomenon of stress, we have looked more closely at syllables as the domain of stress, and we have mentioned that in syllable-sequences some syllables get preferential treatment—they are stressed. In this unit we will explore how syllables and stress combine together into patterns of their own: *rhythm*.

▶ ## TASK 42

Take the word 'extraordinary' again. Said in isolation it contains six syllables. The following words also have six syllables:

internationally

computerization

anti-establishment

One of them is more 'similar' to 'extraordinary' than the others. Which one, and in what way?

Words which have the same rhythm, i.e. the same sequence of stressed and unstressed syllables, sound more like each other.

As a general definition of the word 'rhythm' the *Oxford English Dictionary* gives the following: 'Movement marked by the regulated succession of strong and weak elements'. The list of possible 'movements' is very long, and ranges from our heartbeat, the tick-tock of the clock, the sound of footsteps, fingers tapping, to waves beating on the shore or the change of the tides. It certainly seems as if our lives are pervaded by rhythm, even though the rhythm is not necessarily there objectively but may be something we impose. Human beings seem to have a natural tendency to impose rhythmic patterns on the surrounding world.

The overall principle governing the perception of our surroundings as rhythmical is that we notice things as they are foregrounded as 'figures' against a background. In this way, we perceive a pattern of contrasts which is repeated over a period of time.

This principle of 'figure and background' is manifested in language by stress. In the sense that utterances are continuous strings of syllables, the stressed syllables provide the foreground and the unstressed ones the background. Recent approaches to speech rhythm concentrate on this contrast between stress and unstress.

The second factor, time, has given rise to an important and time-honoured division, the division into stress-timed and syllable-timed languages (Pike 1945, Abercrombie 1967). It is said that in some languages *syllables* follow each other at identical time intervals, that is to say these languages allot an equal amount of time to each syllable. Such languages are called syllable-timed. In other languages, *stresses* are said to occur, at equal intervals and these languages are consequently called stress-timed or isochronous—that is to say, stress-pulses occur at regular time intervals, no matter how many unstressed syllables intervene. It is as if the unstressed syllables have to be reduced somehow in order to be able to be 'squeezed in' between one stress-beat and the next.

Put this way, the two basic language rhythms seem discrete enough, and the claim is appealingly simple. It is not surprising, therefore, that the theory of stress-timing has been popular in English teaching (more on this in 8.3). Problems arise, however, once we look for actual perceptual characterizations of the two distinct rhythms. Syllable-timed languages are claimed to have 'a characteristically even, rather staccato rhythm' (Hawkins 1984: 178), while the theory that English has stress-timed rhythm implies that stressed syllables will tend to occur at relatively regular intervals (Roach 1991: 120). The question is, what is the difference between a regular and an even rhythm?

▶ TASK 43

1 Here are some typical stress-timed and syllable-timed languages:

Stress-timed: English, Swedish, Russian, Arabic
Syllable-timed: Spanish, French, Japanese

If your own language is not included here, would you know which group it belongs to?

2 If we accept that both strong–weak contrast and time are equally important for rhythm, which of the two language types, stress-timed or syllable-timed, should then be considered more rhythmical?

If you are not a speaker of any of the languages mentioned here, you may not have been at all sure what your language type is. The rhythm of our own language simply seems to be fairly regular to us.

If we pursue the answer to the second question logically, we are left with a problem. Given that in stress-timed languages the foregrounded items (the stressed syllables) occur at regular time intervals, these languages should be more rhythmical because the two rhythm factors, contrast and time, coincide. Syllable-timed languages, on the other hand, seem to ignore the time factor, so that strictly speaking they should be said to have no proper rhythm at all! This clearly poses a conundrum. Rhythm seems such a pervasive principle that it appears totally counterintuitive to claim that there are human languages without it.

In fact, the division between syllable-timed and stress-timed languages has never been quite accepted among those phoneticians whose native language happens to be syllable-timed. The classification was set up mostly by English-speaking phoneticians to account for language rhythms that were somehow different from English. In a sense, syllable-timing was negatively defined, as being everything which was not stress-timed.

It may be better to abandon the view that syllable-timing and stress-timing are diametrically opposed, and to regard the two types as end-points of a continuum on which languages can also occupy intermediate positions (Dauer 1983). Wherever they appear on the continuum, all languages have a tendency to reduce the vowels of unstressed syllables. However, languages differ considerably in the extent to which they exploit this tendency. English, for instance, exploits it a great deal by reducing both vowel duration and quality. The *duration* of English unstressed vowels is reduced to a fraction of that of their stressed counterparts. The /ə/ in 'a charge' /əˈtʃɑːdʒ/, for instance, lasts 35 milli-seconds, and the /ɑː/ 272 milliseconds, i.e. the /ɑː/ is over seven times as long as the /ə/ (Grosser 1983, Adams 1979). The quality of the unstressed vowels tends to gravitate towards the neutral /ə/, which has the effect of making schwa the most frequent English sound. Apart from schwa, there is a rather limited set of vowels in English for unstressed syllables to choose from. Other languages may have a larger set of vowels which can occur in unstressed syllables, or they may simply reduce duration but not change the vowel-quality (for example, Italian). We can thus say that 'stress-timed' languages maximize the difference between stressed and unstressed syllables, while 'syllable-timed' languages do not.

5 Intonation

5.1 The nature of intonation

We have been looking at different ways in which human sound is processed. The point to emphasize, of course, is that all this is done in order to communicate. And when we communicate using sounds, we clearly do a good deal more than simply string allophones together to make up words. The messages we convey depend just as much on *how* we say something as on *what* we actually say.

The most obvious aspect of pronunciation is the articulation of specific sounds. Thus, the proper name 'Henry' can be said to consist of a sequence of sounds, or segments, transcribed as /ˈhenri/. But this segmental transcription does not, of course, tell us very much about the way this word might be uttered in any specific situation.

▶ TASK 44

> Think of as many different ways of saying 'Henry' as you possibly can. In order to do this, it may help you to imagine specific situations, and to exaggerate wildly. List these pronunciations using labels which describe their characteristic features. Do not worry about terminology, words such as 'soft' or 'high' are perfectly adequate.

When producing all these different renderings of 'Henry', you presumably did not just vary the individual sound segments. Instead, at least some of your decisions will have concerned the whole word, that is to say, you were expressing *supra*segmental features. *Suprasegmentals*, then, are characteristics which extend over entire utterances, whether they are long texts or just one word. If you listed features such as 'loud'/'soft', 'high'/'low', 'up'/'down', 'fast'('short')/'slow'('long'), and perhaps even some label referring to voice quality such as 'breathy' or 'squeaky', you have managed to exhaust a major part of the suprasegmental, or *prosodic*, repertoire of language. We have already discussed one prosodic aspect of speech, namely stress (see **4**). We now consider the closely related phenomenon of *intonation*.

For the study of intonation, the prosodic features of *pitch* (perceptual label for 'high'/'low'), loudness, and length are particularly important, because they work together in giving certain syllables *prominence* over others. We shall return to the relationship between prominence and intonation presently.

Intonation is often defined as speech melody, consisting of different *tones*. Obviously, what melody (song) and intonation have in common is that in both we make our voice go up or down at will, that is to say, the tones depend on the pitch of the voice. A pattern which can perhaps be regarded as halfway between music and intonation is that of the chant. This, as Bolinger (1985: 8) points out, is often used for taunts, as in:

```
                  a
   John-ny          sweet
         has              heart!
```

One important difference, however, between this chant and intonation in language is that the chant is made up of a succession of stable, sustained tones, whereas intonation often has upward or downward moves within the tone, i.e. glides. Imagine, for instance, that you are entering a dark room looking for John; you might take one step into the room and say:

As opposed to the previous example, where 'John-ny' is uttered on one level, uses an upward glide, or rising tone. A different tone might be used in the following situation: Your doorbell rings. Before you open the door you ask, 'Who's there?' and you hear the reply:

Here a downward glide of the voice is used, also called falling tone.

The choices for pitch movement are limited: we can make our voice go up, go down, remain on the same level, or any combination of these. As we have seen in the above examples, the tone we select will depend on what we want to express. This is particularly obvious in one-word utterances such as 'John', where there is no grammar or additional lexis to make the meaning clear.

But we do not always have a choice. There are expressions which are normally used as fixed formulae, with a set intonation. They could be called 'intonational idioms'. For instance, an alternative way of saying 'very quickly' is 'in no time', with 'no' having the highest pitch:

                    no

        in

                        time

The phrase 'for a change' is usually tagged on to the end of a sentence, and is spoken at a low pitch throughout:

                out,

        Let's go

                        for a change.
(examples from Bolinger 1986: 6)

▶   **TASK 45**

Say the following expressions out loud:

You must be joking!

Beats me! (= I don't know).

There's a good girl!

I see what you mean.

So what!

Can you think of more examples of intonational idioms in English? If English is not your first language, also list some intonational idioms in your own language. If English *is* your first language, try and think of a few such idioms in a foreign language you speak.

The above tasks and examples are intended to familiarize you with the most important factor in intonation, that of pitch movement. We shall look next at how this can be described systematically, and what kinds of linguistic information are conveyed by intonation.

Tone units

So far, we have only looked at tones in very brief utterances. But how can we describe intonation in longer stretches of discourse? Obviously, it would not make much sense to attempt to describe the pitch movements in any utterance by simply providing a kind of 'score' for the ups and downs of the voice. This might render a faithful enough representation of pitch movement, but it would not enable us to make any generalizations which we could then apply to other utterances as well. So for learning and teaching about intonation, we need to understand and be able to describe the recurring patterns, and in order to do this we first need a unit of description. To draw a parallel with grammar, we do not just say that a text consists of a succession of words in different arrangements, but we discern conventional categories such as clauses and sentences in accordance with well-defined syntactic criteria. Also, paragraphs and entire texts cannot just have any arbitrary form, but conform to discourse conventions (see Cook 1989, *Discourse*, published in this series).

What, then, are convenient chunks for the description of intonation? This is a question about which there is still a good deal of debate. Most people, however, agree that speech consists of units of one or more syllables which somehow 'belong together'. Returning to our example above, we said that a possible answer to the question 'Who's there?' (ringing the doorbell) is 'John' with a falling tone: J͡oͪn

This utterance consists of one syllable. But John could also reply:

It's ＭE   J͡oͪn

In this utterance, 'John' and 'me' are more prominent than 'It's', and both are spoken with the same falling tone. Most speakers would divide this utterance into two units of information. 'It's me' and 'John'. Broadly speaking, these units are a representation of the speaker's organization of what he or she says. They have been variously called tone units, sense groups, tone groups, or intonation groups. We shall use the term *tone unit* (as does, for instance, Roach 1991: chapter 16).

▶ TASK 46

Consider the following sentence:

> The students who had studied the language thoroughly enjoyed the play.

Note that this sentence is ambiguous only in writing: as soon as you say it out loud you have to decide on a specific reading. Find different ways of dividing this sentence up into tone units and paraphrase the different versions to make their meaning clear.

Obviously, the example in this task is very much a display sentence invented to demonstrate how the placement of tone unit boundaries can remove ambiguities. In real-life discourse, our interpretation is usually sufficiently constrained by the context. When speaking carefully or reading aloud, speakers usually signal tone unit boundaries fairly clearly through pauses and other prosodic devices. This is not necessarily the case in spontaneous speech, due to its less regular nature, characterized by hesitations, false starts, and the like.

Before we can embark on the description of these tones, we need to know on which syllable(s) in a tone unit the pitch movement is realized. The criterion for this is *prominence* (to be discussed in more detail later). We observed above that in the utterance 'It's me, John', 'me' and 'John', because of their communicative value, are more prominent than 'it's'. We also noticed that 'me' and 'John' are the syllables with a falling tone, i.e. the syllables where the pitch movement takes place. Let us look at a slightly longer utterance, also consisting of two tone units:

> They arrived at eight, and they left at two.

Assuming that this utterance is a reply to a question such as 'What about your guests last night?', most people will agree that the syllables marked in SMALL CAPITALS have prominence, and on the tone unit boundary marked //:

> // They ARRIVED at EIGHT // and they LEFT at TWO //

But where are the significant pitch changes? They are on the focal points of the message, EIGHT and TWO. These are called *tonic syllables*, and they constitute the minimum element of the tone unit.

There is a tendency for the tonic syllable to be placed towards the end of clauses and sentences because of the way information is normally distributed in them. For instance, in 'They arrived at eight, and they left at two', the tonic syllable is the last syllable in both tone units. When the tonic syllable does not coincide with the last syllable, then the pitch movement starts on the tonic syllable and continues to the end of the tone unit, as in:

> Have you thought about WRIting to her?

Here the rising tone would normally start on 'WRI-' and go on up to 'her'.

The division into tone units and the pitch movement on the tonic syllable fulfil an important communicative function. Reconsider the example from above, 'It's me, John', spoken as a request to open the door. We said that the utterance consisted of two tone units, and that 'me' and 'John' were prominent syllables with pitch movement. But this is actually only one of two possible interpretations. In the interpretation we have considered so far, 'me' and 'John' refer to the same person, with John identifying himself by speaking. The other possibility would be to have just one tone unit, i.e. no pause between 'me' and 'John', and thus only one tonic syllable, 'me'. Here the speaker is identifying himself, or herself, and addressing John:

// It's

Here the falling tone starts on the tonic syllable, 'me', and is continued over the next syllable.

▶ TASK 47

Consider the following exchange. Read it aloud. Decide which syllables are prominent, what the tonic syllables are, and which pitch movement you use on them:

A: Did you have a nice weekend?

B: Oh yes, it was lovely! We went to Durham. Jane took me to an old-fashioned restaurant, and we went for a long walk by the river.

When we first mentioned the notion of pitch movement, we said that the choices for the human voice are 'down', 'up', 'same level', or combinations of these. But how are these pitch movements categorized for the English language? Phoneticians vary in the number of different contours they work with. Some claim that two are sufficient, others distinguish between as many as seven or eight. All of them use basic tones which correspond to the possibilities we just mentioned: 'down' is a falling tone, 'up' is a rising tone, and 'same level' is a level tone. There is more variation across different approaches in their definition of more complex tones, but all agree that the combinations 'down–up' = falling–rising tone and 'up–down' = rising–falling tone are common in English. For most purposes, the following set of five tones is perfectly adequate:

Fall ↘

Rise ↗

Rise-fall ↗↘

Fall-rise ↘↗

Level —

The notation here is just one of the many that are used; we have already come across a different one in some examples earlier in this subsection. Thus:

John↗ corresponds to ↗John, and John↘ to ↘John.

Functions of intonation

So far, we have established that intonation is used by speakers to convey information, mainly through choice of significant pitch variation. But what sort of information can be conveyed? In Crystal (1987) six functions of intonation are listed:

– Emotional: expression of attitudinal meanings such as excitement, surprise, reserve, etc. (compare Task 44 above)

– Grammatical: marking of grammatical contrasts, such as chunking into clauses and sentences, or contrast between questions and statements; e.g. 'Richard phoned.' (statement—falling tone) vs. 'Richard phoned?' (question—rising tone).

– Information structure: marking of the distinction between what is already known and what is new; for example, if someone says 'I saw a BLUE car', this presupposes that it is already known that a car is being talked about, and 'blue' is the new information.

– Textual: marking of the structure of larger stretches of discourse, such as the distinctive melodic shape which different paragraphs are given in news-reading.

– Psychological: organization of discourse into units that are more easily perceived and memorized, for example, the tendency to divide telephone numbers into rhythmical chunks.

– Indexical: markers of personal identity, and of group membership; for example, members of certain occupations have distinctive ways of speaking, such as preachers, sports commentators, street vendors, etc. *(Crystal 1987: 171)*

▶ **TASK 48**

Consider Crystal's categorization of the functions of intonation. Could you reduce the number of categories without excluding any important functions? How?

Crystal indicates features which most phoneticians would basically agree on, though they may not all use the same terms and emphasize the same functions. In fact, different approaches to the description of intonation vary considerably with respect to what they focus on and which functions they regard as most important. Such variation of emphasis will to some degree depend on which languages are studied and how the function of intonation in discourse is conceived.

5.2 The nature of discourse

Although we are not usually aware of it in our daily lives, spoken discourse is an extremely complex phenomenon whereby meaning is negotiated in the process of interaction. The study of this phenomenon of language in use, of language as a social process, ranges from close formal textual analysis to social psychology. A concept central to the study of spoken discourse is the speech event, or 'culturally recognized social activity in which language plays a specific ... role' (Levinson 1983: 279), such as everyday conversation, sales encounters, university lectures, church services, and innumerable others.

Hymes (1972) maintains that it is possible to describe every speech event with reference to a range of factors, which include: setting (time and space), participant(s) (addresser and addressee), topic (content), channel (spoken or written), and purpose. These components interrelate in complex ways in particular speech events.

Let us look at a short extract from a speech event. In addition to the information we get from the text written down in ordinary, orthographic form, the transcription also offers us indications of prosodic features, such as tone unit boundaries, pitch movement, and pauses. Also, we can tell when people speak at the same time: overlapping utterances are printed one beneath the other. All this narrows down the options as to how the interaction might be read. Prosody, one can say, mediates between the actual linguistic form and the context. Here, then, is the transcript of the extract, with a table explaining the symbols for these prosodic features.

A we're |looking 'forward to ↑BÒNFIRE night| at |LÈAST| the
   |CHÌLDREN ÁRE| – – do you IN|DÙLGE in 'this| –

B oh in · in |SÙSSEX we DÍD| – – I've – in |FÀCT| I |went to 'one
   'last WÈEK| · but it was ·

A t but the · |"Ì don't know 'where we can ↑get any ↑WÒOD from|
   a|part from ↑chopping 'down a ↑few TRÈES| which I |wouldn't
   'like to DÒ| – we |don't seem to 'have very much ↑WÒOD|

B |YÈS| |THÀT's a PÓINT| · |YÈS| – – |M̌| ·

A well I sup|pose if we 'went 'into the PÀRK| we |might col'lect
   a 'few STÌCKS| but it's |not 'quite 'like 'having · "LÓGS| |ìs
   it| – – but I |don't know 'where 'one would ↑GÈT 'this 'from
   HÉRE| – – I er if |we were m · at "HÒME| · |back in the
   MÌDLANDS| we would |KNÒW| if · you |KNÓW| |where we could GŌ|
   and |GÈT all 'these things 'from| but

B |YÈS| |YÈS| · |M̄| – |M̄| · |in ↑SÙSSEX| – in |my VÌLLAGE|
they – |spent the ↑whole of · of · OC↑TÒBER 'building up the
BÓNFIRE| –

A |M̌|

B   yes they |probably 'did it in ↑YÒURS|

A |they had a ↑VÌLLAGE one DÍD they|

B |YÈS|

A |YÈS|

B |YÈS|

A |YÈAH|

B |ÀLL the 'local 'people| – |HÉLPED with it| |put all their 'old
'ARMCHÁIRS and things| |ÓN it|

A |M̌| – |M̄HM| ·

B |used to be about ↑twenty feet ↑HÌGH | ·

A |M̄|

Table of prosodic features
| tone-unit boundary
| first prominent syllable of the tone-unit
`   falling tone
´   rising tone
ˉ   level tone
^   rising-falling tone
ᵛ   falling-rising tone
`´ fall-plus-rise (on separate syllables)
'   the next syllable is stressed
↑   the next syllable is stressed and also steps up in pitch
"   extra strong stress

·   ⎫
ˉ   ⎬ pauses, from brief to long
– – ⎪
– – – ⎭

SMALL CAPS = words containing the tonic syllable

(*Crystal and Davy 1975: 17, 29*)

▶ TASK 49

Consider the transcript above. Make a note of what this excerpt tells you about the following. Also note down *how* you know, i.e. what your evidence is:

- what kind of speech event is taking place?
- what is the topic being talked about?
- what is a likely setting?
- what are the participants' roles and relationships: are they strangers? colleagues? close friends?

You probably found it quite easy to come up with possible answers: the words on the page convey the impression of a friendly, if not exactly bubbling informal conversation. That the participants are acquaintances of fairly equal social status (not strangers, but not close friends either) becomes apparent partly from what they say, but also from the way the conversation is conducted: they feel free to interrupt each other and to overlap, there is an abundance of fillers such as 'm' and 'erm', and *back-channel signals* (or agreement noises, such as 'yes' or 'mhm'). There are also false starts and incomplete constructions, which are characteristic of informal talk.

The way we manage verbal exchanges is indeed very complex, with a great deal of fast processing and fine tuning going on all the time. These are some of the factors which we juggle, seemingly without effort, whenever we engage in a conversation, both as speakers and as listeners:

- *Prominence*: how to make salient the important points we make
- *Topic management*: how to signal and recognize where one topic ends and another begins
- *Information status:* how to mark what we assume to be shared knowledge as opposed to something new
- *Turn-taking*: when to speak, and when to be silent, how (not) to yield the floor to somebody else
- *Social meanings and roles*: how to position ourselves *vis-à-vis* our interlocutor(s) in terms of status, dominance/authority, politeness, solidarity/separateness
- *Degree of involvement*: how to convey our attitudes, emotions, etc.

This list does not, of course, exhaust all the possible ways in which verbal communication can be described. However, it does represent the most important choices that speakers have. In real life the distinctions between the different choices are not at all clear-cut; they happen simultaneously and interact in ways which sometimes make it impossible to tell them apart. So just like any formalization, the above categories are an idealization, an analytic means enabling us to generalize from individual instances.

If we have a closer look at these categories of speaker choices, we can make a further distinction: the first two, prominence and topic management, have to do mainly with the content of utterances, while the last two are closely associated with participant roles, both social and individual. Information status and turn-taking, the two aspects in the middle of the list, combine 'content' elements and 'relationship' elements in a particularly striking way. Discourses may be geared more towards conducting business or towards 'lubricating' social relationships. The terms that have been established for rendering this distinction are 'transaction' and 'interaction' (discussed in **1.2**). Again, we should bear in mind that pure instances of one or the other are very rare; usually a speech event will serve both functions, but to different degrees.

▶   # TASK 50

Arrange the following speech events on a cline from 'primarily transactional' to 'primarily interactional'.

1 Telling a joke
2 Telephoning the tax office
3 Extending condolences
4 Requesting landing permission from air control
5 Engaging in small talk at a reception
6 Giving a safety demonstration on board an aircraft
7 Being interviewed for a new job
8 Buying a train ticket in a hurry.

Of course, individual speech events will differ from one another most obviously in terms of the setting (for example, pub vs. courtroom) and the actual words used to talk about certain topics. In analysing the conversation about bonfire night with regard to factors of the speech event (see Task 49), there was a good deal we could infer from the transcript, after the event as it were. But wherever we are and whoever we may be talking to, about whatever topic, *how* something is said is obviously part of *what* is said.

But regardless of how the different factors link up, the actual here-and-now of the way any conversation is conducted has to be negotiated from moment to moment. So to get the whole picture, we need to look at the negotiation process itself. It is in this process of negotiation that intonation plays the most crucial part.

5.3 Intonation in discourse

In 5.2 and 1.2 we looked at the distinction between interactional and transactional talk. We also said that in any kind of talk, interlocutors need to negotiate various aspects as they go along. These might be subsumed under the general notions of *topic*, *floor*, and *positioning of participants*. These aspects provide us with a structure for this unit, in which we shall look at the crucial role intonation plays in the negotiating process.

There are many descriptions of intonation in English (for example, Halliday 1970; Crystal 1969), but there is one which tackles head-on the factors we have identified as vital for the analysis of ongoing discourse. This is the one developed by Brazil and his colleagues (Brazil 1981, 1985a and b; Brazil, Coulthard, and Johns 1980). In the following we shall therefore focus on Brazil's model and terminology, making reference to other descriptions where this seems relevant.

Topic and prominence

In any utterance, some words are more important than others, or to put it more technically, have more semantic weight. An example of a real-life situation where we exploit this distribution of information is sending a telegram: 'Tom arriving Derby coach station 7.30 pm tomorrow. Please pick up'. As a general tendency (but not as an invariable rule), so-called *content words* (nouns, verbs, adjectives) tend to carry more semantic weight than others, which are termed *function words* (articles, auxiliaries, prepositions). Phonetically speaking, content words are usually more prominent than function words, and this prominence is indicated by a combination of loudness, length, and pitch movement (see 5.1).

In natural conversation, word-class in itself is not a reliable indicator of prominence. When speaking very quickly, people sometimes de-stress some content words because stressed syllables take more time to say. Speaking in a slow, careful style gives us time for more stressed syllables. Prominence interacts very closely with such prosodic features as rhythm (see 4.4) as well as with lexis, syntax, and context.

There is an important difference between word-stress and prominence: word-stress, the highlighting of the salient syllables in polysyllabic words, is relatively stable. Consider the following:

> Arnold went to a specialist shop to buy some old *records*.
> Arnold writes songs and also *records* them in a studio.

That the noun here is stressed on the first syllable, and the verb on the second syllable, is inherent in the language system—it is not a choice the speaker makes (see 4.3).

Prominence, on the other hand, is to a large extent a matter of speaker choice: it is an indication as to what the speaker wants to make salient in the ongoing discourse, a reflection of how he or she views the 'state of conversational play' (Brazil 1985b: 68). What the speaker chooses to highlight depends on the context, the situation, and what has happened in the conversation so far.

▶ ## TASK 51

Say sentences 1 to 4 aloud, giving prominence to the words in capitals. Choose the appropriate paraphrase (A to D) for each.

1 JOHNNY will eat this	A whether he wants to or not
2 Johnny WILL eat this	B not just look at it
3 Johnny will EAT this	C rather than something else
4 Johnny will eat THIS	D not someone else

Try the same thing with the following sentence and write out your own paraphrases: 'Did Henry Miller live in Paris?'

In everyday conversation we are usually not even aware of the subtle ways in which we make important information noticeable to our listeners by lending it prominence, nor of the extent to which we are dependent on prominence as listeners. It is quite revealing, however, to observe ourselves in more 'self-conscious' speaking activities such as reading aloud, where the effort that goes into decisions about prominence becomes more apparent. After all, who has not had the frustrating experience of having an interesting text read to them by someone who 'just didn't understand' what he or she was reading!

▶ ## TASK 52

The following extract from the novel *Lucky Jim* describes a young academic's reflections about the first sentence of an article he has just written. Read it aloud and observe yourself taking decisions as to which words to give prominence to:

Dixon had read, or begun to read, dozens like it, but his own seemed worse than most in its air of being convinced of its own usefulness and significance. 'In considering this strangely neglected topic', it began. This what neglected topic? This strangely what topic? This strangely neglected what? His thinking all this without having defiled and set fire to the typescript only made him appear to himself as more of a hypocrite and fool.
(Amis 1953: 14)

This extract illustrates how important clear indications of prominence are for the (imaginary) listener. What it also demonstrates is that prominence is something crucially dependent on context: the words 'begun', 'what', and 'more' are highlighted by virtue of the function they fulfil in their respective tone units in relation to the other parts.

But how exactly *do* we signal that prominence? What did *you* do, for instance, to highlight the three 'what's in Dixon's questions? There is not just one straightforward answer; in all probability you used some or all of the following to a certain degree: pitch movement, increased loudness, duration, paralinguistic features such as facial expression, and voice quality. Of these, however, pitch movement is the one most closely bound up with prominence. As we said in **5.1**, the major pitch movement takes place, or begins, on the tonic syllable, which is by definition the syllable with the greatest prominence in the tone unit. So the way you read Dixon's questions above probably sounded like this:

> This ⌃WHAT neglected TOPIC? This strangely ⌄WHAT TOPIC? This STRANGEly neglected ⌃WHAT?

The major pitch movement takes place on 'what' in all three occurrences, thus indicating the location of prominence. We could say that by being given prominence the three 'what's are topicalized.

Introducing and ending topics

How do we use our voice to introduce topics, and how do we develop, change, or close them? Consider this short exchange about country life:

> A: but I prefer Sussex er I don't know what the subtle difference in the countryside is but there's something
> B: Yes Sussex has super heath country
> *(Crystal and Davy 1975: 80)*

Speaker B introduces a new mini-topic, 'heath country'. As the tape makes clear, in order to do this, she jumps to high pitch, or high *key* in Brazil's terminology, on the first syllable in the word 'super'. In the notation for prominence and pitch level introduced in **5.1**, B's utterance looks like this:

high			SUper HEATH	
mid	**B:**	// yes // sussex has		country //

There are no absolute values for high, mid, and low key: 'high' therefore means high compared to the immediately preceding tone unit. It is interesting to note that the move to high key is also often employed for those so-called 'little words' which we use to mark off the boundaries of topical sequences, such as '*right*, how about a drink ...', or '*okay*, where are those books you want me to return ...'. Here is an example from classroom discourse, where high key is the teacher's signalling device for the beginning of a new sequence:

high	NOW	beFORE i came to		
mid	//	//	SCHOOL // this MORning ... //

(Brazil, Coulthard, and Johns 1980: 66)

(Since capitals are used for prominent syllables, the first person singular pronoun 'I' is printed in lower case in these examples when it is not prominent.)

Conversely, low key is often used to mark the ending of a topical segment, as in

mid   // WELL THAT'S IT then   //   //
low   THAT'S FInished
(McCarthy 1991: 112)

The jump to high key and the drop to low are realized on the first prominent syllable of the tone unit. Recent research indicates that these pitch phenomena can in fact be much more important than the (more obvious) lexical criteria for the marking of topic boundaries (Coulthard 1992: 48).

Rather than looking at key choices in terms of the opening, continuing, or ending of topics, one could say more generally that relative pitch level can be used to indicate relationships between successive tone units. Thus the second tone unit in the following example will have a different informational value according to whether it is uttered at mid, high, or low key:

	GOT it:	*high key*
she APPLIED for the JOB // and	GOT it:	*mid key*
	GOT it:	*low key*

A jump to high key will usually be interpreted as emphatic, maybe contrary to expectations; continuation on mid key simply adds information by stating that she both applied for the job and got it; low key, on the other hand, carries the meaning 'as you would expect'. The terms used for the meanings added by these key choices are contrastive (high), additive (mid), and equative (low) (see Brazil 1985a: chapter 3; Coulthard 1985: 111ff).

Floor and turn-taking

So far we have only talked about key with reference to one-speaker utterances. But these relationships also hold between successive utterances of different speakers in turn-taking, such as in question-answer sequences.

Turn-taking, then, is the way in which speakers hold or pass the floor (Cook 1989, *Discourse*: 52ff., Bygate 1987, *Speaking*: 39ff., published in this series). Competent speakers achieve efficient turn-taking, with very precise timing, by taking into account many factors simultaneously: syntactic and lexical signals, eye contact, body position and movement, loudness, and intonation. The fact that turn-taking mechanisms also work on the telephone, however, suggests that vocal paralinguistic factors such as pitch and loudness are particularly important.

▶ ## TASK 53

Consider the following exchange between a policeman (P) and a witness (W). Observe the beginnings and endings of each turn: where is pitch likely to be relatively high, and where relatively low?

P: Did you get a look at the one in the car?

W: I saw his face, yeah.

P: What sort of age was he?

W: About 45. He was wearing a ...

P: And how tall?

W: Six foot one.

P: Six foot one. Hair?

W: Dark and curly. Is this going to take long? I've got to collect the kids from school.

P: Not much longer, no. What about his clothes?

W: He was a bit scruffy-looking, blue trousers, black ...

P: Jeans?

W: Yeah.

(Fairclough 1989: 18)

Intonation, or more precisely the factor of key or pitch height, is one important cue indicating a speaker's desire to continue his or her turn, or willingness to give it up. Non-low pitch is normally a signal for wanting to hold a turn, and low pitch for yielding it (Cutler and Pearson 1986). In the above extract, the fact that the exchange is an unequal encounter controlled by the policeman is reflected, among other things, in the fact that he interrupts the witness twice. If you compare the way you hear the ending of W's last (completed) turn with that of her (interrupted) last-but-one, you should find that 'black' is in higher key than 'yeah'.

Intonational turn-taking cues can overrule syntactic ones. Brown, Currie, and Kenworthy (1980: 189) observed speakers who uttered a complete sentence and might be expected to have finished their turn, but who used non-low pitch at the end of their utterance to indicate that they wanted to hold the floor.

In a sense, the opposite happens when speakers use back-channel signals ('m', 'yes', 'm-mhm') as in this short extract from the conversation discussed in 5.2:

B: in Sussex in my village they spent the whole of—of October building up the bonfire

A: m

B: yes they probably did it in yours

A: they had a village one did they
B: yes
...
B: all the local people helped with it put all their old armchairs and things on it
A: m-mhm

It is essential that speakers should use low pitch for these 'agreement noises' in order to signal that they are not bidding for a turn, but that they are listening and taking in what the other person is saying. Key is a matter of conversational co-operation between speakers.

Positioning of participants: social meanings and roles

As we have seen from our discussion of topic management and turn-taking, the way intonation signals informativeness and helps lubricate conversational mechanisms is always bound up with roles the participants play in this interaction, and with the way they perceive these roles and acknowledge them in subtle intonational choices. This becomes particularly apparent when we look at how tone, or pitch movement, operates in conversation.

In order to do this, let us start with the already familiar extract from *Lucky Jim*:

This ⁄WHAT neglected TOPIC? This strangely ⋁WHAT TOPIC? This STRANGEly neglected ⁄WHAT?

We said that when reading these questions aloud, speakers would mark the 'what's as the tonic syllables and would most probably use end-rising tones.

Now, if we consider the six functions of intonation mentioned by Crystal (1987: 171) and quoted in 5.1 on page 49, the rising tone on Dixon's 'what's could be due to almost any of these functions: for example, the emotional function could be to express disbelief, annoyance, impatience, or something similar. The grammatical function could indicate that these utterances are questions rather than statements. The problem, however, is that not *all* rising tones signify disbelief, annoyance, or impatience, nor do *all* questions have rising intonation. It is simply impossible to establish any such straightforward one-to-one relationships between particular semantic and syntactic elements on the one hand and particular tone contours on the other.

A still widely-used description of (British English) intonation by O'Connor and Arnold (1973) attempts to correlate syntactic forms with certain tone contours and associate specific speaker attitudes with these combinations. For instance, they say that a certain kind of falling tone (1) makes statements more 'categoric, weighty, judicial, considered' (1973: 48); but on the other hand, the same tone is also said to (2) 'give weight to expressions of both approval and disapproval, of both enthusiasm and impatience' (1973: 49).

▶ ## TASK 54

Consider the following examples from O'Connor and Arnold (1973: 49ff) illustrating the attitudinal meanings described above. Which ones do you assign a meaning from group (1) above, and which from group (2)? What are your criteria for deciding?

(Are you sure?) Absolutely ＼certain.

(Can't we do something?) You must be ＼patient.

I entirely a＼gree with you.

I hope it'll be a ＼lesson to you.

It was perfectly ＼wonderful.

(How do I look?) Absolutely ＼ravishing.

Since you had no auditory criteria or paralinguistic information (such as gesture or voice quality), nor indeed any context to go by, you really had no choice but to assign meaning to the above examples according to the semantic meanings of the lexical items constituting them. But the assignment of certain meanings, such as attitude or syntactic category, to certain tones does not really help us to go beyond *ad hoc* observations; in other words, it does not allow us to make valid generalizations (for a discussion of this problem see Coulthard 1985: chapter 5).

By contrast, David Brazil's (1985a and b) model of the 'meaning' of tone contours in British English works with a limited set of possible choices. Brazil's system is of particular interest to us here because it focuses on the communicative value of intonation in the 'state of play' in discourse as it is negotiated moment by moment by the interlocutors. Brazil's approach thus seems to be compatible with the current concern with observing interaction from the participants' point of view.

For interaction to be possible at all, there needs to be some common ground between the interlocutors. 'Common ground' does not just mean 'shared knowledge' or 'something already mentioned', but, as Brazil, Coulthard, and Johns put it,

'[common ground] is intended to encompass what knowledge speakers (think they) share about the world, about each other's experiences, attitudes and emotions ... It may be helpful to think, in diagrammatic terms, of the speaker seeing his world and the hearer's as overlapping,

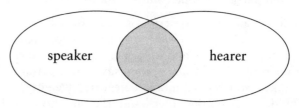

and to see him as faced, as he composes, with a moment by moment decision as to whether what he says can be assumed to be shared or not.'
(Brazil, Coulthard, and Johns 1980: 15)

It is precisely this assessment as to what is shared and what is not that determines the speaker's choice of tone. According to Brazil, the major opposition here is between end-falling tones ⌄/⌃ and end-rising tones ⌄⌃. Of these, the fall ⌄ and the fall-rise ⌄ are the most frequent. This is to say that in RP intonation the unmarked, i.e. 'neutral' instance of an end-falling tone is ⌄, and the unmarked instance of an end-rising tone is ⌄. (If ⌃ or ⌃ are chosen instead this has certain social implications, which we shall come to presently.)

How, then, are falling and rising tones employed in talk? For a part of the message which the speaker regards as part of the existing common ground, he or she will use ⌄. For a tone unit which he or she sees as adding to the common ground, he or she will choose ⌄. Brazil has introduced the terms *referring* (r) for ⌄ and *proclaiming* (p) for ⌄. Here is an example:

> // (r) what we <u>COULD</u> DO // (p) is go OUT for a <u>MEAL</u> //

The r tone on the first tone unit indicates that the question as to what the interlocutors could do together has already arisen. The choice of the p tone on the second tone unit indicates that the information is presented as new.

▶   TASK 55

Match the questions below with the corresponding answers. Think about what the speakers seem to consider common ground (r ⌄) and what is seen as adding to the common ground (p ⌄).

1 When do you want to travel the world?
2 Why do you turn the radio on before leaving the house?
3 What do you do before leaving the house?
4 What do you want to do when you finish school?

A (r) When I finish school // (p) I want to travel the world.
B (r) I want to travel the world // (p) when I finish school.
C (r) I turn the radio on // (p) so as to scare off burglars.
D (p) I turn the radio on // (r) before leaving the house.

We can see here that answer D, for example, is given in a situation where the notion of leaving the house has already been introduced (question 3). In natural conversation, of course, it is often only the 'p' part of the answer which is given, the one which adds new information.

The negotiation of common ground is central to Brazil's model. He argues that what his system captures at the most general level could best be characterized in social terms:

'In making the referring choice, the speaker invokes the togetherness aspect of the conversational relationship, speaking as it were for the "we" who are the participants. In making the proclaiming choice, he adopts the stance of the "I" who is set over against the "you" in a situation of unassimilated viewpoints.'
(Brazil 1985b: 68).

Continuing the theme of social roles and relationships signalled by choices of tone, we can now turn to the meanings conveyed by tones which diverge from the unmarked distribution of referring and proclaiming tones. Consider, for instance, expressions such as 'actually', 'frankly', or 'surely', which are often employed to evoke solidarity, agreement, or intimacy, as in:

// (r)HONestly // (r) i've ALWAYS FOUND him a bit STRANGE //

In this example, 'honestly' clearly does not provide any new information, since being honest is regarded as the conversational norm and therefore does not need to be mentioned specially. However, 'honestly' can also be used to express divergence, lack of agreement, or distance. In order to signal this meaning, the speaker would choose a falling tone which proclaims this attitude:

// (p)(but) HONestly // (p)you're being unFAIR //

So far we have only looked at r ∨ and p ↘. But according to Brazil, speakers have two choices each for referring and proclaiming tones. These are shown in Figure 1.

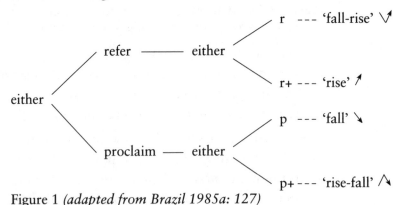

Figure 1 *(adapted from Brazil 1985a: 127)*

The tones r+ and p+ are the less frequent, that is to say marked, versions of r and p. What further significance, then, is attached to the tonic segment by employing these marked choices?

Brazil and his colleagues (Sinclair and Coulthard 1975, Sinclair and Brazil 1982) examined a great deal of so-called non-symmetrical verbal encounters involving dominant and non-dominant participants, such as conventional school lessons and doctor–patient consultations. They observed that what typically happens in such encounters is that the non-dominant parties, such as pupils and patients, only use r and p tones, while the dominant parties, such as teacher and doctor, have a choice between r and r+, and p and p+. Thus, r+ and p+ are regarded as dominant-speaker choices. They tell us about the way role relationships are perceived by the interlocutors, and indicate which speakers have, or claim, dominance over the other(s). *Dominance* is thus a technical term used by Brazil to indicate the amount of control a speaker has over the development of the discourse. This control concerns decisions as to who speaks when, and what is spoken about. Compare, for instance, the following two utterances:

a. // (r) WHEN i've finished what i'm DOing // (p) i'll HELP you //

b. // (r+) WHEN i've finished what i'm DOing // (p) i'll HELP you //
(Brazil 1985a: 133)

The difference between (a) and (b) could be made explicit by paraphrasing:

a. 'If you wait a minute, I'll help you'

b. 'If you want me to help you, you'll have to wait'

Utterance (a) might, for instance, be used by a child offering help to an adult, whereas (b) used by a child might well be regarded as insolent. An adult, on the other hand, 'would normally be considered to have the choice between being accommodatingly helpful (r tone) and regulatory (r+ tone)' (Brazil 1985a: 134). In other words, the adult would be the dominant speaker in this situation. The marked version of the proclaiming tone, p+ ╱╲ , is relatively uncommon and, according to Brazil, it also tends to be exploited by a dominant speaker. The choice of tones·can thus be seen to be an important factor in negotiating social relationships, including those of power and solidarity.

In general, then, Brazil's notion of dominance, in the sense of freedom to make linguistic choices, seems to be a particularly powerful explanation of the significance of intonation in discourse, precisely because of its generality. However, it might be said that its very generality also creates problems for pedagogical application. Brazil's analysis of the p+ tone is based on distinctions which may be too subtle to survive in practical teaching. There may also be difficulties in deciding just when and why a speaker feels entitled to make use of dominant choices. It may well be that in most teaching situations, it is enough for learners to be able to distinguish p+ from other tones, not necessarily to learn how and when to produce it. In fact, for some learners it might be important to learn to *avoid* using p+ if their linguistic background causes them to over-use the p+ tone in English. Roach (1991: 139ff.) refers to the rise-fall as not important for foreign learners to acquire. Even Bradford (1988), an excellent book on intonation practice based entirely on Brazil's model, leaves out p+.

The main problem, then, about describing tones in a way which is adequate for learners of English is to steer a course that is neither too specific nor too general. It seems that teachers should get across to students a number of crucial points about the way intonation functions in discourse. One is that intonation is the most important means by which interlocutors negotiate their mutual relationship and indicate how they view the topic under discussion. Another is that during the interaction, intonation enables participants to constantly check and establish common ground in order to achieve convergence and conversational solidarity. Kenworthy (1992) offers more details on this as well as excellent suggestions for classroom activities.

Demonstration

6 Pronunciation teaching

In Section One we discussed a number of issues concerning the description of speech. We distinguished between the phonetic or physical aspect and the phonological or psychological aspect (sounds in the body and sounds in the mind), and between segmental and suprasegmental features. The question we need to address now is how this description of sound, the domain of the *disciplines* of phonetics and phonology, is relevant to the *subject* of language teaching, and in particular, of course, to the pedagogy of pronunciation teaching.

6.1 Relevance

The first and most general point to be made is that it is always an advantage, indeed one may claim it is a necessary requirement, that teachers of a language should know *about* the language they are teaching.

Practical proficiency is not enough; if it were, then anybody able to speak a particular language would be qualified to teach it. But pedagogic competence does not necessarily follow from linguistic competence, since it involves the ability to identify specific aspects of language, to select and combine them for presentation and practice in ways which are effective for learning.

If the teacher can only exemplify pronunciation by his or her own speech performance, the learners are left to work out what is significant for themselves. Learners of a second or other language will not readily discern crucial phonological distinctions.

Even if they do discern them, they may not be able to imitate them in their own speech. Some learners, it is true, are naturally gifted mimics and will 'pick up' a pronunciation by exposure. Many, perhaps most, however, need to have their attention drawn to what they have to do by explicit explanation. Making learners notice things by consciousness raising is as crucial to pronunciation as it is to the teaching of other aspects of language such as grammar and vocabulary.

▶ TASK 56

Consider the following fictional account of a father trying to teach his son how to pronounce a particular sound in his own language. Would you follow this procedure for teaching pronunciation in a second language, and if not, why not? What questions do you think the passage raises about the teaching of pronunciation in general?

'Ernest,' said Theobald from the armchair in front of the fire where he was sitting with his hands folded before him, 'don't you think it would be very nice if you were to say "come" like other people instead of "tum"?'

'I do say tum' replied Ernest, meaning that he had said 'come'.

. . .

'No, Ernest, you don't,' he said, 'you say nothing of the kind, you say "tum" not "come". Now say "come" after me, as I do.'

'Tum' said Ernest, at once; 'is that better?' I have no doubt that he thought it was, but it was not.

'Now, Ernest, you are not taking pains: you are not trying as you ought to do. It is high time you learned to say "come", why, Joey can say "come", can't you, Joey?'

'Yeth, I can,' replied Joey, and he said something which was not far off 'come'.

'There, Ernest, do you hear that? There's no difficulty about it, nor shadow of difficulty. Now, take your own time, think about it, and say "come" after me.'

The boy remained silent for a few seconds and then said 'tum' again.

. . .

'Now, Ernest. I will give you one more chance, and if you don't say "come", I shall know that you are self-willed and naughty'.

He looked very angry and a shade came over Ernest's face, like that which comes upon the face of a puppy when it is being scolded without understanding why. The child saw well what was coming now, was frightened, and, of course, said 'tum' once more.

(from Samuel Butler, The Way of All Flesh *1966: 124ff.)*

One obvious thing that this fictional incident can be said to illustrate is that teaching by intimidation is not only morally undesirable, but ineffective as well. But apart from this, we might note too that Ernest does not seem to *hear* the sound at issue, let alone pronounce it for himself. So there is no point in simply repeating the sound to him and ordering him to imitate it, for it does indeed fall on deaf ears. These two sounds /k/ and /t/ are both voiceless stop consonants: the difference between them is a simple matter of place of articulation. With even a little rudimentary knowledge of phonetics, Theobald would be more likely to achieve his objective—by telling his son what to do with his tongue.

But what of the objective itself? This raises the issue not of *how* but *what* pronunciation should be taught. Why is Ernest required to pronounce this particular sound? It is not because he would otherwise be incomprehensible, since Theobald knows that by 'tum' he means 'come'. It is evidently so that he can sound 'like other people'—the people his father takes as providing a proper model of linguistic behaviour. He believes that it is 'high time' for Ernest to conform to received pronunciation with respect to this particular sound. Joey, by the way, can get away with his non-conformist consonant /θ/ in 'Yeth' (instead of /s/ as in 'Yes'). That sound is not (not yet at least) one which Theobald decides is to be stigmatized.

We can link this to the more general question of what serves as an appropriate model for pronunciation teaching. If the pronunciation of a particular sound does not interfere with communication, should it be corrected? Theobald wants Ernest to conform to 'other people', that is to say the people in a particular community of speakers. Should we try to get our students to conform in the same way? And if so, which community should provide us with the pronunciation model?

This piece of fiction, then, is relevant to our concerns in that it raises two major considerations for language pedagogy: what *approach* to the teaching of pronunciation is appropriate (which we will take up in 6.2), and what *model* should we set up for the students to conform to (which we considered in 1.1)?

6.2 Approaches to teaching

We can talk about approaches to teaching pronunciation (and the teaching of other things) by reference to selection—how the items to be taught are to be defined—and presentation—how they are to be actually taught in the classroom.

With reference to *selection*, we can, very generally, place different approaches along two dimensions. One of these has to do with the size of the unit which is given precedence: whether it is the separate segment of sound (as discussed in 2) or the larger prosodic unit (as discussed in 4 and 5). In the first case, we have a bottom-up approach, beginning with the articulation of individual vowels and consonants and working up towards intonation. In the second case, we have a top-down approach, beginning with patterns of intonation and bringing separate sounds into sharper focus as and when required. Clearly, a particular direction (bottom-up/top-down) is not likely to be rigidly adhered to throughout an entire course: different purposes and stages in learning call for different priorities.

Nevertheless, these directions do carry with them a very general pedagogic assumption about dependency which it is important to note, namely that certain aspects of pronunciation need to be overtly taught to provide the conditions whereby other aspects are covertly learned. In the bottom-up approach, the basic idea is that if you teach the segments, the suprasegmental features will take care of themselves. This has obvious parallels with a structural approach to teaching the grammatical and lexical features of language. In the top-down approach, the assumption is that once the prosodic features of pronunciation are in place, the necessary segmental discriminations will follow of their own accord. This view is consistent with a more communicative perspective in language teaching, in that it focuses on how speakers achieve meaning in discourse.

▶ ## TASK 57

For English, Bryan Jenner has suggested the following list of priorities (in order of importance not in sequence for teaching). How could this be used to devise a course suitable for the needs of your students?

1 The consonantal inventory

2 Vowel quantity: i.e. long and short

3 Syllabic structure: i.e. closed with clusters

4 Syllabic values: strong, weak, reduced

5 Rhythmic patterning: 'stress-timing'

6 Prominence and tonicity: i.e. location of pitch features

7 Tones: *some* binary opposition, such as fall vs. fall-rise

8 Articulatory setting: laxity and lack of movement

9 Vowel quality: all vowels should be drawled. The details of shape then follow

10 Pitch levels: high, mid, low

(11 Voice quality, if the learner's native habits are disturbingly different from those of native varieties of English).
(Jenner 1989: 4)

A second dimension has to do with whether the focus of attention is primarily on where the students are coming from or where they are going to. In the first case, pronunciation teaching will, as a matter of priority, be concerned with possible first language interference, with the filter effect which we referred to earlier, and teaching will tend to concentrate on those aspects of pronunciation which are likely to present difficulties for particular groups of learners, given their linguistic background. In the other case, the focus will be on target-language behaviour, and there will be a tendency to concentrate on those aspects of speech which are more functionally significant in actual language use. Again, a particular set of materials may well vary along this dimension at different stages. Or it may be that a particular course shows no signs of having taken this dimension into account at all.

These two dimensions are shown in Figure 2.

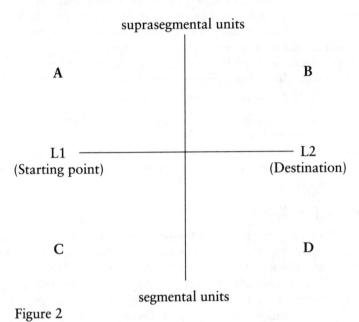

Figure 2

▶ **TASK 58**

Consider any set of teaching materials you know, or the activities for pronunciation teaching you use yourself, and see where you would put them on this diagram. If they are based on the individual sounds which particular students find difficult because of their first language, for example, they would appear in quadrant C.

With reference now to presentation, we can (again very generally) distinguish three kinds of procedure: exposure, exercise, and explanation (see also Stern's (1992: 120) 'implicit'–'explicit' range of procedures for teaching pronunciation).

In the *exposure* procedure, spoken language occurs contingently in the context of some task or other activity which motivates the use of language.

No explicit attention is paid to the specific features of pronunciation, segmental or suprasegmental. The assumption is that because the use of language is motivated by some communicative purpose, sounds will be heard as significant and will be learnt as such.

By *exercise* we mean the traditional procedure of identifying specific sound features and providing practice in perception and production. What distinguishes the exercise (in our terms) is that if focuses quite specifically on form (segmental or suprasegmental).

Both exposure and exercise procedures are based on the belief that students will be able to use the input for intake (Corder 1981) and learn the distinctions presented to them, either by inference or imitation. With *explanation*, the assumption is that this will not necessarily happen unaided, and that it can be helpful to make students consciously aware of phonetic, and phonological, facts. With *explanation*, the kind of knowledge about the sounds of speech that we presented in Section One of this book is put to direct methodological use.

Obviously, these different procedures can combine in various ways: one does not preclude the other. What is important is to establish which procedures, in which combinations, are appropriate for particular features of pronunciation, particular purposes, and particular students.

▶   **TASK 59**

Identify what kind of procedures are used in the materials and activities you are familiar with. Do you find that there are instances where other procedures, or combinations, would have been possible/more appropriate for your classroom? Do you think there are approaches to language teaching in general (structural, communicative, etc.) which favour one kind of procedure rather than another?

6.3 Teachability–learnability

As we emphasized in Section One, pronunciation, more than any other aspect of a foreign language, will always be influenced by very personal factors such as the learner's attitude to the target language and to the speakers of that language, by individual differences in ability and motivation to learn, etc. This may be the most important reason why, especially in pronunciation, there can never be a one-to-one relationship between what is taught and what is learnt. It would be self-defeating for the teacher to think or hope that there ever could be.

For pedagogical purposes, it might in fact be helpful to think about the various aspects of pronunciation along a teachability–learnability scale. Some things, say the distinction between fortis and lenis consonants, are fairly easy to describe and to generalize—they are teachable. Other aspects, notably the attitudinal function of intonation, are extremely dependent on individual circumstances and therefore nearly impossible to isolate out for direct teaching. Peter Roach warns us that:

'... of the rules and generalizations that could be made about conveying attitudes through intonation, those which are not actually wrong are likely to be too trivial to be worth learning ... the complexity of the total set of sequential and prosodic components of intonation and of paralinguistic features makes it a very difficult thing to teach ... The attitudinal use of intonation is something that is best acquired through talking with and listening to English speakers...'
(Roach 1991: 168ff.)

In other words, some aspects might better be left for learning without teacher intervention. An advantage of this is that it allows more scope for learner initiative.

However, there seems to be a conundrum for pedagogy here: prominence, tones, and key (as discussed under Intonation in 5) are particularly important in discourse, in that they allow speakers to negotiate their relationships and to indicate how they view the topic under discussion. At the same time they are particularly difficult to teach. With individual sound segments it is the other way round: they are relatively easy to teach, but also relatively less important for communication. There thus seems to be an inverse relationship between communicative importance and teachability, as shown in Figure 3.

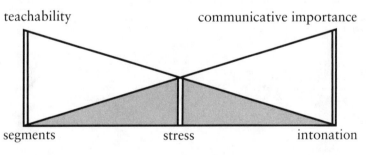

Figure 3

If we think in these terms, however, we can identify an area with maximum overlap of communicative importance and teachability. This is stress.

It may be, then, that work on stress is the most convenient focal point for any course in pronunciation. It is necessarily connected to either end of the continuum: on the segmental side, word-stress is decisive for the quality of individual sounds, on the intonation side, it signifies prominence.

One disadvantage of focusing on linguistic form (whether in grammar or pronunciation teaching) is that learners have difficulty making the language real and responding to it in a natural way. In actual speech (be it dialogues, or reading aloud) this often results in learners suspending any involvement with what they are saying or reading, as if to signal 'this is not my text'. The effect of this suspension is a kind of mechanical speech style, characterized by very flat intonation and lack or misplacement of stress. Working on stress first can have the desirable effect of persuading learners to think about what *they* find important and what they want to convey as salient—to make the text their own.

7 Focus on intonation

7.1 Intonation teaching: important but (too) difficult?

There can be no doubt about it: intonation is a crucial element of verbal interaction, and most authors of teachers' handbooks and teaching materials agree on this. Presumably, then, the communicative importance of intonation should also be reflected in the attention it gets in language teaching. Morley, reporting on a large TESOL (Teachers of English to Speakers of Other Languages) colloquium on pronunciation, says that participants agreed on the desirability of

'a focus on the primary importance of suprasegmentals (i.e. stress, rhythm, intonation, etc.) and how they are used to communicate meaning, with a secondary importance assigned to segmentals (i.e. vowel and consonant sounds).'
(Morley 1987: Preface)

It is interesting to note, however, that in the same volume, in a contribution entitled 'Teaching pronunciation as communication', Celce-Murcia remarks:

'The one glaring omission in my current approach is that I am still having problems with fully integrating stress and intonation in my teaching of English pronunciation.'
(Celce-Murcia 1987: 11)

Coursebooks, both general English courses and special pronunciation textbooks, often seem to have similar problems: even when other aspects of pronunciation are dealt with thoroughly, intonation is usually given short shrift, or left out altogether.

▶ TASK 60

Consider these two statements, which both deal with the question of whether it is worth 'bothering' with intonation.

'Unlike grammar, vocabulary, and segmental pronunciation, mistakes in intonation are not usually noticed and allowed for by native speakers, who assume that in this respect a person sounds as he means to sound. "That chap has some interesting things to

say, but he's so arrogant about it all" may be a reaction to a foreigner who has little control over his low rising tones, for
instance. This kind of unconscious brick-dropping is, we know,
extremely common; and its eradication should be a main aim of
any approach to the teaching of conversation.'
(Crystal and Davy 1975: 8)

'I no longer explicitly teach intonation to general classes, though I
teach it implicitly in "say this after me" exercises. My direct
efforts to get students to use English (i.e. mainly my own) intonation were not rewarding: 1. Some students seemed to feel that a
change in their personalities was being attempted; 2. Some—the
mimics or actors—repeated the patterns accurately, but seldom
used them in their free conversations, except where the patterns
more or less coincided with those in their own L1 speech. 3. I find
it difficult to mould my intonation to that in textbooks ... ; the
subjective element is too strong. No doubt my students had a similar problem. 4. I felt that un-English intonation did not interfere
seriously with my perception of students' meanings, feelings and
attitudes: my "adaptor" worked quite well, as did their adaptors,
it seemed.'
(Barnes 1988: 17)

Which of these quotations do you find it easier to relate to?
Which factors can you identify in these statements that are relevant for the decision to teach, or not to teach, intonation? What
is your own opinion on this question, and with reference to which
criteria?

The above statements represent opposing points of view, though clearly
both are tenable and feasible in certain situations. They mention many
factors which need to be taken into account when deciding on a particular approach to teaching intonation. These include (in Crystal and Davy
1975) the question of models and norms (see **1.1**), social messages conveyed, mostly subliminally, by intonation patterns, and beliefs about the
correlation between teaching and learning. In the quotation from
Barnes, the factors mentioned include: explicit vs. implicit teaching,
kinds of courses and future needs of students, the teacher as *one* model,
learner types, and the role of the native language.

We seem, then, to be confronted with a somewhat paradoxical situation:
on the one hand, there is widespread consensus about the significance of
intonation for successful communication; on the other, intonation is the
'problem child' of pronunciation teaching, for materials writers and
teachers alike (see also **6.3**).

When looking at suggestions for teaching in a variety of materials, our
objective will be to identify possible sources of confusion and to try to
make visible the underlying commonalities which can serve as a basis for
a broad consensus.

One source of confusion is the variation across teaching materials as to what gets treated under the heading 'intonation'. For instance, we demonstrated in 5.3 that pitch movement and prominence are inextricably bound up, but some materials deal with these phenomena quite separately. In these cases, 'intonation' refers exclusively to patterns of pitch movement such as rising and falling contours, and prominence is dealt with under such headings as 'sentence stress' or '(sentence) rhythm'.

In this book, we have chosen to take the functions of intonation as the starting points, i.e. to look at what intonation *does* when people talk, and to look at the various *forms* which serve to fulfil these functions. Opportunities for receptive and productive work on intonation abound in *any* spoken language activity: an important ability that teachers need is to recognize and take advantage of these opportunities with reference to the priorities that will best serve the interests of their learners.

7.2 Ways into intonation

Considering the communicative importance of intonation on the one hand, and its largely subliminal nature which makes it difficult to describe and teach on the other, sensitizing and awareness-raising activities are particularly important.

For instance, intonation is often referred to as 'vocal gesture'. Getting learners to explore gestures may indeed serve as a fun way into language-specific work on intonation. Suggestions for this are more likely to be found in general coursebooks and in materials for conversation than in specialized pronunciation books.

▶   TASK 61

The following pictures from *Conversation* (Nolasco and Arthur 1987) are used to raise awareness about the significance of gesture. How might they be used as a warm-up to the teaching of 'vocal gesture'? What are the most important insights you would expect your students to gain through a discussion of gestures? What kinds of tasks would you devise to make the transition from gestures to intonation? For example, could any of these gestures be replaced by vocalizations?

(Nolasco and Arthur 1987: 64)

Nolasco and Arthur point out that using these pictures is likely to generate particularly interesting discussion in a multilingual class. Whatever the composition of the class, however, it is important for learners to realize that gestures—and also 'vocal gestures'—are conventional in nature, that is, they convey certain messages to members of certain communities. Some gestures may well be the same across various communities, some may lend themselves to a number of interpretations within a community, while some may cause incomprehension or bewilderment. The same observations might be made about aspects of intonation.

In **5.1** we mentioned the analogy between music and intonation, which is often referred to as speech melody. This comparison may be helpful in explaining the concept of intonation, but it does not alter the fact that many learners, even musical ones, find it extremely difficult to perceive where the speaker's voice goes up and where it goes down, let alone to control pitch movement consciously in their own speech. This is overlooked in some textbooks, which plunge straight into the practice of falling and rising tones. There may be a real danger here of 'losing' one's students at this stage, and of creating anxiety which may get in the way of further learning.

▶ **TASK 62**

Consider the intonational idioms in Task 45, or any of your own examples. Can you think of activities or techniques which can serve as a gentle way into attuning learners' ears to the pitch movement in them?

The suggestions made in various textbooks include such techniques as humming the tune instead of using words. Gilbert (1993a) recommends the use of a kazoo, a cheap toy humming instrument. Both these 'tricks' have the advantage of dissociating pitch from words or syntax, and so make it easier to perceive. Wong (1987) favours 'minimal dialogues' such as the following, which students listen to and then interpret:

He: Ready? ↗

She: No. ↘

He: Why? ↘

She: Problems. ↘

He: Problems? ↗

She: Yes. ↘

He: What? ↘

She: Babysitter. ↘

(Wong 1987: 62)

Another good starting point which is intuitively accessible to many learners is the 'chunking' of utterances into tone units. We said in **5.1** that tone units reflect the speaker's organization of the message through the assignment of prominence to certain syllables and pitch movement.

▶ **TASK 63**

In Judy Gilbert's *Clear Speech* (1993a), two out of the three units entitled 'Intonational' deal with 'thought groups', which is her term for tone units. Try out the activity overleaf. Work in pairs if possible so that you can check whether the listener arrives at the correct answer.

C

Pair practice: arithmetic

1 Student 1 says either (a) or (b) with a pitch fall at the end of each group. The new group starts on a higher pitch. This shows the listener the beginning and ending of the group. Student 2 says the answer. The correct answer depends on correct grouping.

▭ Examples $(2 + 3) \times 5 = 25$
two plus three times five equals twenty-five

$2 + (3 \times 5) = 17$
two plus three times five equals seventeen

1. a. $3 \times (3 + 5) = 24$
   b. $(3 \times 3) + 5 = 14$

2. a. $(5 - 2) \times 2 = 6$ (five minus two)
   b. $5 - (2 \times 2) = 1$

3. a. $(4 - 1) \times 3 = 9$
   b. $4 - (1 \times 3) = 1$

(Gilbert 1993a: 109)

What did you observe 'Student 1' doing in order to mark off thought groups? Do you find this activity effective?

Gilbert (1993a: 108) defines thought groups like this:

'A thought group is a group of words that belong together. There are two main signals to mark the end of a thought group: *pause* and *falling pitch*.'

You may have found when trying out the activity yourself that you did not use both these signals, but maybe only pauses, and maybe even rising rather than falling pitch for some groups. For students at an early stage, it may in fact be enough to become sensitized to the important 'signposting' function of pauses and to realize that tone units are not directly related to grammatical units such as sentences.

The above exercise gives learners immediate feedback: 'Student 2' can only get the sums right if 'Student 1' uses pauses in the appropriate places. Unlike grammar or lexis, pronunciation, and intonation in particular, is an area of language teaching where notions of linguistic correctness are not helpful. More than in other areas, the only real measure of success is the degree to which the intended message and the perceived message overlap. Therefore, the opportunity to check on the communicative outcome of utterances, as demonstrated in this arithmetic task, is a particularly valuable asset of activities on suprasegmental aspects of pronunciation, and a criterion worth bearing in mind when evaluating practice materials in this area.

7.3 Foregrounding

Maybe *the* most important function of intonation, and almost certainly
the most teachable one, is the signalling of prominence achieved through
a combination of pitch, loudness, and extra vowel length (as discussed
in **5.3**). Coursebooks refer to this phenomenon with a variety of terms,
such as 'highlighting' (Bradford 1988), 'focus' (Gilbert 1993a), 'tonic
prominence' (Bowen and Marks 1992). In some publications we also
find the term 'sentence stress'—which, as Roach (1991: 172) reminds us,
is not an appropriate name, since prominence does not concern the
grammatical unit of the sentence, but the tone unit.

In **5.3** we said that prominence is very much a matter of speaker choice:
by emphasizing certain words more than others, the speaker makes these
more noticeable to the hearer and so 'steers' the way the message will be
understood.

▶   **TASK 64**

When working with students on prominence, do the materials
you use offer the learners the opportunity to make motivated
choices with regard to prominence, or do they just require purely
phonetic manipulation? Compare the following activities from
two textbooks:

Extract 1

> B. *Now practise shifting the Tonic yourself:*
>
> (a) Are you coming to Majorca with us this *summer*?
>   Are you coming to Majorca with us *this* summer?
>   Are you coming to Majorca with *us* this summer?
>   Are you coming to *Majorca* with us this summer?
>   Are *you* coming to Majorca with us this summer?
>   *Are* you coming to Majorca with us this summer?
>
> (b) *My* wife doesn't look like a sack of potatoes.
>   My *wife* doesn't look like a sack of potatoes.
>   My wife *doesn't* look like a sack of potatoes.
>   My wife doesn't *look* like a sack of potatoes.
>   My wife doesn't look like a *sack* of potatoes.
>   My wife doesn't look like a sack of *potatoes*.
>
> C. *Can you add something to each sentence to explain the implication
>   of the change of stress in the sentences in Question B?*

(Ponsonby 1987: 80)

Extract 2

> *4.4.* For this activity work with a partner if possible. B uses the same
> words to respond to the two different things that A says.
>
> i) A: Paul looks happy!
>   A: I think Paul needs a new car.
>
>   B: He's got a new car.
>
> ii) A: We must get some flowers.
>   A: Don't forget to get them a present.
>
>   B: I've got some flowers.
>
> iii) A: Let's go to Paris.
>   A: Have you had a good weekend?
>
>   B: I've been to Paris.

(Bradford 1988: 9)

The activity from Bradford's *Intonation in Context* may seem difficult at
first, but by the time learners are asked to do it, they are already familiar
with the pattern of practice from a preceding guided listening exercise,
which looks like this:

> *4.1* Listen to the following utterances: you will hear each one twice.
> Decide which of the questions, (a) or (b), provides a suitable con-
> text for what you hear. The highlighting is not transcribed here, so
> you must recognise which word is made prominent.
>
> i) They hired a car.
>   a) Did they take the car?
>   b) Did they hire bikes?
>
> ii) No, the train was delayed.
>   a) Had she already arrived at the station?
>   b) Was the plane late?
>
> iii) The bank's on the corner.
>   a) Where's the bank?
>   b) What's on the corner?

(Bradford 1988: 7)

7.4 New information and common ground

Speaker choices as to which message parts to foreground and which to background depend on which parts we expect to be new to the hearer, and what we assume to be common ground. We have seen in **5.3** that intonation is the primary means by which interlocutors simultaneously negotiate their relationship and indicate the way they view the topic under discussion. They do this, broadly speaking, by using referring tone (∨✓) for common ground and proclaiming tone (↘) for new information.

As we said in **5.3**, this explanation of tone choice is a very general one, which has the advantage that it points to underlying regularities which do not become evident in other, less unified, approaches.

▶   # TASK 65

Consider these two activities aiming to practise the use of certain tones. For both, the relevant explanatory text preceding them is given as well.

Extract 1

> (a) As well as serving to make prominent the accented words in an utterance, intonation may also distinguish different types of sentence and different attitudes of the speaker.
>
> (b) In the following sections, examples will be given of such sentence-types as:
>
>   (1) statements
>   (2) WH questions (i.e. questions beginning with such words as 'when', 'why', etc.)
>   (3) Yes/No questions (i.e. questions expecting the answer 'yes' or 'no')
>   (4) commands, warnings, requests
>   (5) exclamations, greetings
>
> (c) Some alternative attitudes likely to be implied by various intonation patterns are given brief verbal descriptions in each case, but it must be remembered that the precise attitudinal connotation of intonation patterns will always depend upon the contextual situation in which they occur ...

I 29 *Listen and repeat*
(___ ‿): routine; lack of interest; surly
‚This is ‚mine.
You can ‚come on ‚Tuesday.
I'd ‚like some ‚tea.

I 30 *Listen and repeat*
(⎯ ‿): lively; enthusiastic; forceful
'This is ‚mine.
You can 'come on ‚Tuesday.
I'd 'like some ‚tea.

I 35 *Listen and repeat*
(___ ‚): reserved; unenthusiastic; grudging
‚This is ‚mine.
You can ‚come on ‚Tuesday.
I'd ‚like some ‚tea.
It's ‚all ‚right.

I 36 *Listen and repeat*
(⎯ ‚): reassuring; lively; polite; unfinished
'This is ‚mine.
You can 'come on ‚Tuesday.
I'd 'like some ‚tea.
It's 'all ‚right.

I 40 *Listen and repeat*
(ˋ ˇ): strongly assertive + encouraging, lively, reproachful;
also implying an alternative
You can ˋcome on ˇTuesday.
I'd ˋlike some ˇtea.
‚John ˋgave me a ˇbook.

I 47 *Listen and repeat*
(‚): curt; detached; routine
‚Where? ‚How? ‚When did you ‚come?

(Gimson 1975: 60ff.)

Extract 2

The tones

i) THE FALL (↘)
Speakers use falling tones in parts of utterances which contain information they think is new for their hearers – when they are *telling*
them something they don't already know. It may be information in
response to a question, e.g. Gill: ... [↘] we could give her a book.
Or it may be information the speakers present as new, something
they want their hearers to know about or consider, e.g. Dave: [↘]
What shall we give Claire?

ii) THE FALL-RISE (↘↗)
Speakers use fall-rise tones in parts of utterances which contain
ideas they think their hearers already know about or have experience of. They *refer* to something shared by themselves and the hearers at that point in the conversation. It may be something they both
know about, e.g. Gill: [↘↗] Well, as she likes reading ... Or it may
be something which has just been stated or implied in the conversation.

4.2 Listen to this example:
B: // ↘↗I'm GOing to the THEatre // ↘on SATurday//
This is a suitable response in a context like this:
A: Let's go to the theatre.
B: // ↘↗I'm GOing to the THEatre // ↘on SATurday//
where the theatre is an idea already shared by A and B.

Now go on in the same way. A and B have finally arranged to
meet. But they haven't decided what to do. Whatever A suggests B has either done already or is going to do it soon.

i) A: Let's go to the sports centre, then.
    B: // ↘↗   // ↘toMORROw //

ii) A: Would you like to see a film?
    B: // ↘↗   // ↘this EVEning //

iii) A: Shall we visit Janet? She keeps inviting us.
    B: // ↘↗   // ↘next MONday //

iv) A: We could try the new Italian restaurant.
    B: // ↘↗   // ↘last SATurday //

v) A: Why don't we drive to the coast?
    B: // ↘↗   // ↘on THURSday //

vi) A: Well let's just stay in and listen to some music.
    B: // ↘↗   // ↘LAST night //
    That's what we always do in the end!

Bradford 1988: 12, 15–16

Compare the two extracts on pages 83–5.

1 Which is the more general and which the more particular?

2 Which can you relate to the functions of intonation as presented in 5.3?

3 Which would you choose for working on these tones with your students, and why?

Extract 1 will probably look familiar to many readers. It is an example of the time-honoured method of relating certain syntactic patterns (statements, yes/no questions, etc.) and attitudinal labels ('reproachful', 'lively') to certain tones. Undoubtedly there are advantages to this, for instance that attitudes and emotions are intrinsically interesting, and syntactic patterns are a reassuringly familiar category for many learners. On the negative side, as Gimson himself points out in the above extract, the attitudinal connotation of intonation patterns is extremely context-dependent, and therefore impossible to generalize and predict. It therefore seems desirable to rely on a broader, more general and therefore more reliable framework, even at the danger of it being too general for certain purposes. This is where the strength of Bradford's approach lies: the dichotomy between telling and referring tones does not overwhelm learners with a plethora of minute distinctions.

▶ **TASK 66**

Can you reinterpret some of the examples from Gimson in the previous task with reference to the telling–referring distinction used by Bradford?

Bradford (1988) is the only intonation textbook to date which consistently deals with tones by referring to new information and common ground rather than relating them to attitudes or grammatical features. Of course, many language teachers do not have the time for a great deal of intonation teaching and may never use a specialized pronunciation book, let alone a textbook exclusively devoted to intonation. This is why a broader, more powerful approach can be especially valuable to teachers as a frame of reference for the selection of intonation activities which take into account how people interact in discourse.

7.5 Managing conversation

Topic

Relative pitch height on prominent syllables, or key choices in Brazil's terminology, indicates the informational value of successive tone units: high key for contrast, mid key for addition, low key for 'more of the same' (see **5.3**).

In this framework, key is a system of basically three choices, each of which has a definable meaning. It would therefore seem desirable to have materials which lead learners to an understanding of how these three choices operate in discourse. However, in most teaching materials there is no indication at all that key constitutes a system with functionally distinct categories. In fact, the only key choice for which exercises are normally provided is the contrastive one, under such headings as 'contrastive' (or 'corrective') stress.

▶   TASK 67

The following activity comes from *Headway Pronunciation: Upper-Intermediate* (Bowler and Cunningham 1991). It is to be found in a sub-unit entitled 'Vocabulary of literature', with a presentation of the relevant literary terms and their pronunciations immediately preceding the extract below. How could this exercise be used to practise the production of contrastive key?

T.4.5.   Listen and practise saying the words. Look at the phonemic transcript as you say each one.

2   The following sentences have some mistakes in them. Can you correct them?

Possible answers:

a. Hans Andersen wrote some wonderful science fiction stories.

a. Jules Verne wrote some wonderful science fiction stories.

b. The hero of the book is a girl called Alice.

b. The heroine of the book is a girl called Alice.

c. Anthony Burgess's autobiography of Shakespeare is an interesting book.

c. Anthony Burgess's autobiography is an interesting book.

d. Oscar Wilde was the narrator of *The Picture of Dorian Gray*.

d. Oscar Wilde was the author of *The Picture of Dorian Gray*.

e. The last chapter of the opera—when Mimi dies in front of her helpless friends—always brings tears to my eyes.

e. The last scene of the opera—when Mimi dies in front of her helpless friends—always brings tears to my eyes.

f. *Venus and Adonis* is a famous rhyme by Shakespeare.	f. *Venus and Adonis* is a famous poem by Shakespeare.
g. The conversation in Oscar Wilde's plays is always very good.	g. The dialogue in Oscar Wilde's plays is always very good.
h. Mickey Mouse is a very famous cartoon hero.	h. Mickey Mouse is a very famous cartoon character.

(Bowler and Cunningham 1991: 24, 91)

If activities such as this one are to be used for practising contrastive high key, learners' attention should be drawn to the fact that the contrast is expressed not simply through loudness or drastic pitch movement, but primarily through the move up in pitch from mid to high on the prominent syllable, for example:

<u>VERNE</u>

jules   wrote some wonderful science fiction stories

Since key is a system with three functionally distinct categories, learners should also be made aware of the meanings conveyed by mid key and low key. For mid key, it will suffice to point out that this is usually the neutral or unmarked choice. In order to bring out the differences between high and low key, the best pedagogical strategy will often be to offer students utterances in which both key choices are possible, and to ask them to match them with appropriate discoursal contexts. Here is an example adapted from Brazil, Coulthard, and Johns 1980:

In this exercise, the choice of *high* or *low* key in the second tone unit of the item is the focus of our attention. Match the utterances with high (a) or low (b) key with the appropriate inferences (i) or (ii):

<u>GAR</u>dening
(a) // our <u>NEIGH</u>bours // are   //
(b) // our <u>NEIGH</u>bours // are   //
<u>GAR</u>dening

(i)   The neighbours are fanatical gardeners.
(ii) The neighbours normally neglect their garden.

<u>BANK</u>er
(a) // i met henry's <u>BROTH</u>er // he's a   //
(b) // i met henry's <u>BROTH</u>er // he's a   //
<u>BANK</u>er

(i)   Henry's family are well-known for their financial interests.
(ii) Henry's family are mostly pretty inept when it comes to money matters.

(Brazil, Coulthard, and Johns 1980: 34ff.)

It is also possible to provide practice in the production of low key without contrasting it. In conversation (but also in other speech events such as lectures or interviews, for example in the media), self-paraphrasing is quite common—that is to say, speakers tend to restate what they have just said in different words, usually in low key: this phenomenon, which makes the 'equative' meaning of low key especially clear, is exploited in Bradford 1988:

▶ **TASK 68**

How would you use the following activity to practise the use of low key?

4.1 Listen to this short utterance and then try to say it in the same way.

We couldn't get in; there were no tickets left.

Now go on. Read these utterances and lower the pitch of your voice when you get to the part which is the same in meaning as what precedes it.

i)   Heat the oven to 400 degrees fahrenheit – that's 200 degrees centigrade.

ii) He's studying at the University of California, in Los Angeles.

iii) Just as I got to the station the guard blew the whistle and the train left.

iv) Please fasten your seat belts – we're about to land.

(Bradford 1988: 36)

This activity can also be used to illustrate to students that knowing where to use low key is important: with utterances (iii) and (iv) in particular, inappropriate key choice, i.e. high instead of low, would not only mislead listeners but might even produce quite a comical effect!

Key is also important in the way people manage conversation: high key can be a signal for the introduction of a new topic sequence, and low key can serve to indicate that the speaker has finished with a topic. This is why key can serve as a turn-taking cue in conversation.

Although key choices are so crucial and all-pervasive as a device for conversation management, there seem to be hardly any published intonation materials that concentrate on this resource. But precisely because of the all-pervasiveness of this phenomenon, it is easy enough to make your own. In fact, you only need to recognize the opportunities available in practically any dialogue.

▶   TASK 69

Consider the following extract taken at random from O'Connor
and Fletcher's *Sounds English*:

🔊 **4.1. Listen and practise this conversation in a shop.**

A: I'm looking for a raincoat, please.
B: Yes, of course. They're over here, on the left. There's been
rather a rush today. Now, what about this blue one?
A: No, the blue is too bright.
B: But blue suits you.
A: Really? I think I look terrible in blue. I'd rather have a brown
raincoat. There was one in the front window that was rather
attractive.
B: I'm sorry, that's the only brown one left, and it's a very large
size. Do you like yellow? This yellow one is the right size.
A: No, not yellow. Have you only got blue and yellow?
B: I'm afraid so. This year the fashionable colours are brown,
cream, blue and yellow. The brown and cream raincoats have all
been sold already, so there's only blue or yellow left.
A: Right! I think I'll try the shop across the road.

(O'Connor and Fletcher 1989: 57)

1 What do you think the objective of the activity is? (The book
title is a clue!)

2 Can you see a way in which you can use this dialogue for
exploring with your students the distinction between high key
for signalling a new topic as opposed to mid or low key choices
for continuing a topic?

This extract is in fact intended for practising the sounds /l/ and /r/. But
since these are presented in the context of a dialogue, the practice will
inevitably involve intonation as well. Consider, for instance, B's first turn
in response to A's request for a raincoat. If there is a point in having a dialogue at all (rather than, say, minimal pairs), then we should expect normal
discourse conditions to operate. Thus, speaker B will need to take a decision
about key on 'rush': the remark about the rush could be interpreted as continuing the same topic—as a kind of explanation—in which case mid or
even low key would be appropriate. If, however, this remark is understood
to be about a different topic (in which case it might seem rather odd), high
key would be the appropriate choice.

Floor

Let us briefly now consider how pitch height is used to ensure the
smooth management of floor—the way speakers bid for a turn, or give
up their turn to another speaker. This works in harmony with topic
management.

Again, there seem to be no intonation materials which address this directly, but opportunities abound in any quasi-natural conversation. Here is an extract from a book which has hardly any explicit coverage of intonation, but which can be used for the teaching of this feature:

► **TASK 70**

Could you use this dialogue from *Telephoning in English* (Naterop and Revell 1987) for work on key as a turn-taking cue?

RON BENSON RINGS BACK

Tom Parker:	703129. Parker speaking.
Ron Benson:	Is that you, Tom. It's Ron. I said I'd phone you back.
Tom Parker:	Ah, Ron. Sorry I disturbed you before.
Ron Benson:	Oh, that's OK. You couldn't have known that I had someone here then. Listen, you wanted Maria Edwardes' address, didn't you?
Tom Parker:	Yes, have you got it?
Ron Benson:	Mm, here it is. Miss Maria Edwardes – Edwardes spelt E-D-W-A-R-D-E-S, 18 Dones Street, Cavite City, Manila.
Tom Parker:	Thanks a lot. May I just repeat it? Maria Edwardes, Edwardes with an E at the end, 80 Dones Street, Cavite...
Ron Benson:	No, it's eighteen, not eighty.
Tom Parker:	OK, 18 Dones Street, Cavite City, Manila. Well, thanks again. Sorry to have troubled you.
Ron Benson:	Not at all. You're welcome. Hope to see you again soon. Bye then, Tom.
Tom Parker:	Bye Ron. Take care.

(Naterop and Revell 1987: 90)

The dialogue above is a transcript from the tape accompanying the telephoning course. It can be used to demonstrate to students how the interlocutors drop their pitch when they yield the turn, or conversely, how the pitch is at a different height when a speaker gets interrupted in full flight as in '80 Dones Street, Cavite...'

Another example of key as turn-taking cue is the low pitch level at which back-channel signals (such as 'mhm', 'yeah', etc.) have to be delivered in order not to be mistaken for interruptions. Activities for practising this feature could be devised from extracts of natural conversation such as the one in **5.2** (pages 50–1).

7.6 Roles, status, and involvement

We have already looked at how speech melody, or tone, functions in the foregrounding and backgrounding of information. Some closely related aspects of spoken interaction, in which tone choice also plays an important part, are the roles, status, and involvement of speakers. It is this area of tone choices which is most readily associated with the term 'intonation'. At the same time, tones are also what many teachers find most confusing, most difficult to systematize, and therefore nearly impossible to teach.

Most activities teaching intonation contours do so in terms of attitudinal meaning, in a manner similar to the example in **5.3** from O'Connor and Arnold (1973), which is a kind of prototype (see page 60). Typical labels used for categorizing and explaining tone choices include 'amazed', 'censorious', 'impulsive', 'sympathetic', 'tactful'. To illustrate tone choices, these labels are usually associated with certain syntactic categories (statements, *wh*-questions) and/or language functions, such as 'giving advice', '(dis)agreeing', 'complaining'.

▶ TASK 71

Here is a very brief extract from Hill's *Stress and Intonation Step by Step*:

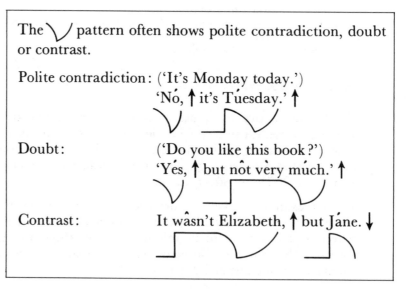

(*Hill 1965: 88*)

What does this extract attempt to teach? Do you think it is likely to enable students to transfer the criteria illustrated for choosing this particular tone to other situations?

The extract seeks to demonstrate that in a specified context, a particular tone contour may be interpreted as conveying a particular attitude. It may be valuable to be able to do this, but there are also problems: above all, the attitudes or intentions of speakers are never signalled by intonation alone. Thus, the notion of politeness is bound to be relative and situation-specific. Coursebooks which present intonation contours simply for imitation, without specifying discoursal context or contrasting them with other possibilities, only offer limited guidance to learners.

▶ ## TASK 72

Consider again the exchanges in the example in the preceding task. When reading out the responses you will probably find that they may well have a fall-rise, but that a falling tone is also possible. The fall-rise thus only gives us one situation-specific rendering, tied to a particular situation.

Can Brazil's notions of proclaiming and referring tone (see page 61) be applied to place this exchange in a more general framework and relate it to other utterances with the same tone choice?

In Brazil's framework, we could relate tone choice to assumptions of common ground between speakers. The response 'No, it's Tuesday' could thus be read, with a fall-rise, as referring to something which the speaker actually assumes to be known to his or her interlocutor (though temporarily forgotten). Alternatively, 'No, it's Tuesday' could also be said with a falling tone, proclaiming 'something new'. In this case, the message conveyed may well be 'I know better than you', making this tone choice less face-saving, and thus less polite, than acknowledging shared knowledge by using the referring ∨ tone. Which tone is actually chosen will depend on factors specific to the situation, the relationship between the speakers, and how they view the topic under discussion. But the criteria which lead to either referring or proclaiming tone are general, and learners can subsequently apply them to their 'own' situations.

What this brief discussion of the above example is meant to demonstrate, then, is that the local meanings ascribed to specific instances can usefully be seen in a global framework of a few significant contrastive choices, which will allow for more productive teaching.

Tone choice is also relevant for signalling status. In 5.3 we said that the two main tones used in English are the fall ↘ and the fall-rise ∨, but that there is also a dominant speaker choice for referring tone, namely ↗. This tone can be used by the speaker who has, or is claiming, dominance in a conversation. In terms of intonation contour, dominant speakers (that is, speakers with high status or speakers in a forceful, assertive role) have the choice between r (∨) and r+ (↗) tones, whereas for non-dominant speakers only r is appropriate.

▶ ## TASK 73

Compare the following activities for practising the ↗ tone. Can you rephrase the explanations offered to learners in such a way that you formulate one explanation which is applicable to both?

Extract 1

---

6 **Drill Six. This is a test drill. You will have one in every lesson. First you will listen to a short conversation, then you must answer questions about the attitudes of the speakers. You have now studied two attitudes, 'polite and friendly' and 'asking someone to repeat part of their remark'. Now listen to a short telephone conversation.**

Hello. Is that Bill?
ˋYes.
This is Helen. How are you?
ˋFine.
Do you know, I met Christopher yesterday.
ˊWho.
Christopher. He told me he'd got a new job.
ˊWhat.
He said he'd got a new job. Quite surprising.
ˋYes.

Now you will hear the conversation in short sections. Answer the question after each section. Then I will tell you the right answer.

Hello. Is that Bill?
ˋYes.

Is Bill polite and friendly or is he asking Helen to repeat?
He's polite and friendly.

This is Helen. How are you?
ˋFine.

Is he polite and friendly or is he asking her to repeat?
He's polite and friendly.

Do you know, I met Christopher yesterday.
ˊWho.

Is he polite and friendly or is he asking her to repeat?
He's asking her to repeat.

(Cook 1968: 4–5)

Extract 2

Part IV: Intonation Patterns That Change the Meaning

(a) She's a doctor.	Intonation can change the meaning of sentences. Study the following examples:
(b) She's a doctor?	(a) a statement of fact (b) echo question, or statement of surprise or disbelief

Exercise 13: Production

Part A: Put a dot over the information focus in each sentence. Then practice saying each one, first as a statement, and then as a question, or if you like, as a statement of surprise or disbelief. (For the latter, you will need to take it to pitch level 4.)

  Example: He left.   He left?

1. The hike starts at 6:00 A.M.

2. My check bounced

3. This is what you wanted

4. There's a mid-term next week

5. We're finally finished with this

6. My fever's 102°

7. We have to take a taxi

8. Class has been cancelled

Part B: Work with a partner. One person reads each sentence, either as a statement or as a question. The other listens and says "Oh" or "O.K." if it is a statement. If a question, the response is "That's right."

(Hagen and Grogan 1992: 136 and 137)

Both these activities illustrate, among other things, so-called echo questions, but without offering a generalizable rationale as to why these questions should have a rising tone. Cook's example conveys the message that there are systematic choices between using a falling tone for sounding 'polite and friendly' and a rising tone for 'asking for repetition'. Apart from constituting a rather surprising opposition, these options lack any relation, or contrast, with the ∨ tone. Hagen and Grogan basically offer the same, namely an exercise in the recognition and manipulation of ↘ vs. ↗, without giving explicit reasons for choosing ↗ rather than ∨.

The most important objection from a pedagogic point of view would seem to be that some of the examples we considered above may offer accurate and very interesting observations, but they are unlikely to engender further learning. For learning to take place, students need to be able to make valid generalizations from individual cases. In order to do this, they have to understand a finite set of criteria or guidelines from which to extrapolate to different situations. Purely incidental approaches based on a multitude of examples are more likely to confuse learners, or to encourage faulty generalizations.

Teachers need to give their learners some guidance on intonation. Recent work has, in principle, provided such guidance. In it, intonation has been increasingly integrated with models of discourse analysis which emphasize context and speaker choice. However, teaching materials currently in use still tend to draw upon more traditional accounts which have a way of fixing intonation patterns too rigidly and without reference to context. This state of affairs shifts a great deal of responsibility onto the teacher, who will need to inform him- or herself about intonation in the language he or she is teaching, and exploit teaching materials accordingly. The decision as to whether and how to tackle intonation will depend on, amongst other things, the specific needs of the learners and on the teaching situation.

Whether or not this decision entails the explicit teaching of certain aspects of intonation or not, it would certainly be desirable to foster in learners a general understanding of the processes involved in verbal interaction along the lines we suggest in this book. Such a sensitization of learners to the communicative role of intonation may prepare their minds for further learning when the limits of teaching have been reached.

8.1 Identifying and producing stressed syllables

Our discussion in Section One showed that stress is a universal phenomenon. We also saw that its perception is due to the combined effect of various factors such as loudness, pitch, duration, and quality. Furthermore, the exact weighting of the different factors is language-specific, with loudness generally playing a lesser role than one would expect. The complexity of the stress phenomenon, and the interplay of its different components, has for a long time discouraged textbook writers from paying due attention to it. As far as pronunciation coursebooks are concerned, stress has only recently come to figure more prominently on the agenda.

▶ TASK 74

Consider the two extracts. Which of the explanations is more consistent with our discussion in **4.1**?

Extract 1

Syllable Stress
'In words of more than one syllable, the syllables do not all have equal stress. There is usually one that has particularly strong stress. This means that on this syllable your voice is louder and usually pitched higher, and you hang on to the syllable considerably longer than on the other syllables of that word. Different stressing can change the meaning of a word or make it completely unrecognizable.'
(Ponsonby 1987: 14)

Extract 2

Stress
'In English some syllables are much more prominent than others. This prominence, or stress, is important to make speech clear. There are three main signals of stress:

1 Pitch change

2 Length of syllable

3 Vowel quality

Together these signals make syllables sound louder'.

(Rogerson and Gilbert 1990: 11)

Extract 2 raises awareness of the importance of stress for clear speech in general. Extract 1, while also singling out the factors involved in syllable stress, limits the issue immediately to the question of word-stress and thus to a specific (lexical) function of stress. In fact, this is the way in which stress is introduced in nearly all textbooks that pay attention to the issue at all.

▶ **TASK 75**

Consider the following exercise on word-stress from the first unit of a general English course. What do you think is the main point of the exercise?

---

5 **Pronunciation: stress. Listen and repeat.**

☐ ▫   ☐ ▫ ▫   ▫ ☐

England   Italy   Japan
English   Germany   Chinese
Britain   Switzerland
British   ▫ ☐ ▫ ▫
German   ▫ ▫ ☐   Italian
China   Japanese   American
                          Australian

(Swan and Walter 1984: 9)

This technique is probably successful in pointing out that in English word-stress can fall in different places (as opposed to Czech, for example, where stress generally falls on the first syllable), while underscoring learners' intuitions about the 'strength' of stressed syllables. Wong (1987) suggests that work on stressed syllables should be more explicit than this. In view of the fact that syllable duration seems to play a far more important role in English than in many other languages (see **4.1**), this seems to be a good idea. Wong's suggestion exploits kinaesthetic experience (the simultaneous activation of different sensations such as hearing and movement) to achieve this.

▶ **TASK 76**

Do you think the kinaesthetic experience offered here can help in learning to pick up the differences between stressed and unstressed syllables?

1 Take a set of 3-syllable words such as 'oranges', 'pineapples', 'computer'. Mark the syllable lengths and ask students to note the differences in length as they listen to you reading each one.

2 Before the second reading, distribute rubber bands to each student. Show them how to stretch the rubber band with their two index fingers according to the length of a syllable. Try it with

'banana'. They should stretch the band a little for ba, more for na, and a little again for na. Exaggerate on the longer syllable: stretch—STRETCH—stretch.

(adapted from Wong 1987: 26–7)

Since the major discrepancies between native and non-native syllables tend to lie in the *duration* of the *unstressed* ones, this is a particularly important issue to address.

For the purpose of teaching the difference between stressed and unstressed syllables we have two alternatives: we can concentrate on the stressed syllables (as exemplified in Task 76) or we can concentrate on the unstressed ones. Baker (1981) employs a conveniently simple technique for conveying that important changes happen in unstressed syllables. In a normally typeset reading text, unstressed vowels are replaced by the schwa sign /ə/.

Barbərə spent Satəday aftənoon looking ət ə beautifəl book about South əmericə.

'I want tə go tə South əmericə,' she said tə həself.

The next morning, when Barbərə woke up it wəs six ə'clock, ənd hə brothəs ənd sistəs wə still əsleep. Barbərə looked ət thəm, ənd closed hər eyes əgain.

Then she quiətly got out əf bed ənd started tə pack hə suitcase.

She took səme comfətəble clothes out əf the cupbəd. She packed ə pair əf binoculəs ənd hə siste's camərə. She packed ə photəgraph əf həself ənd one əf hə mothər ənd fathə.

'I mustn't fəget tə have səme breakfəst,' she said tə həself. Bət then she looked ət the clock. It was ə quartə tə seven.

'I'll jəst drink ə glass əf watə,' she said.

'ə glass əf watə,' she said.

'Watə,' she said, ənd opened her eyes.

(Baker 1981: 44)

▶ **TASK 77**

Here are two activities for working on weak syllables. What order would you present them in? Why?

– point out that weak vowels are mostly transcribed as /ə/ and then ask learners to look up the pronunciation of certain words in a dictionary

– tell learners that you will read out a list of 15 two-syllable words and ask them to write down in each case '1st' or '2nd' according to which syllable they hear as containing a weak vowel.

Here, as in practically every other area of pronunciation, learners need to *perceive* differences before they can be expected to produce them. It may be a good idea to start listening for schwa without the written version of the words, in order to avoid interference from spelling. The written word can then be introduced at a later stage. The written form may discourage learners from weakening unstressed vowels as they may be reluctant to 'mispronounce' their vowel-letters. With more advanced students it is therefore a useful eye-opener (or rather ear-opener) to ask them to count all the vowel sounds in a stretch of text. Ask them, as a second step, to work out how many of them are realized as schwa. As a rule of thumb, about a third of the vowels will be schwa, with a great variety of spellings.

8.2 Prediction skills for word-stress

In **4.3** we said that in many languages word-stress patterns, especially the location of the stressed syllable, are crucial for the smooth processing of the spoken language. There are numerous anecdotes about misunderstandings created through misplaced word-stress:

▶ TASK 78

Here are two such cases. What went wrong and why? Can you add your own anecdote(s)?

1 Student to English literature tutor: 'What do you think about /əˈniːmɪzm/ in *King Lear*?' Tutor wonders about the connection between anaemia and Shakespeare's play. (*Brown 1990*)

2 Host introducing a guest speaker: 'Professor X is a very /ˈɪmpɒtənt/ man in the field of ...' (embarrassment and giggles).

What the speakers meant was, of course, 'Animism' and 'impORtant'. On the whole, coursebooks acknowledge that English word-stress needs attention, but they differ in the way they present it.

One way of dealing with word-stress is simply to include the information in a wordlist and expect learners to memorize the stress pattern of a word together with its meaning, its spelling, and its sounds. This is the information we get when we look up words in a dictionary.

▶ TASK 79

Here is an excerpt from the *Oxford Advanced Learner's Dictionary (4th edition)*. What are the advantages and disadvantages of learning word-stress by this approach?

---

in·ter·ment /ɪnˈtɜːmənt/ *n* (*fml*) [C, U] burying of a dead body. Cf INTER.

in·ter·mezzo /ˌɪntəˈmetsəʊ/ *n* (*pl* ~s or -zzi /-tsɪ/) (*music*) (a) short composition to be played between the acts of a drama or an opera, or one that comes between the main movements of a symphony or some other large work. (b) short instrumental piece in one movement: *two intermezzi by Brahms.*

in·ter·min·able /ɪnˈtɜːmɪnəbl/ *adj* (*usu derog*) going on too long, and usu therefore annoying or boring: *an interminable argument, debate, sermon, etc.* ▷ in·ter·min·ably /-əblɪ/ *adv*: *We had to wait interminably.*

in·ter·mingle /ˌɪntəˈmɪŋgl/ *v* [I, Ipc, Tn, Tn·pr] ~ (sb/sth) (with sb/sth) (cause people, ideas, substances, etc to) mix together. *Oil and water will not intermingle.* ○ *a busy trad-*

The advantage is that most learners have access to a dictionary and use it frequently; by looking up a lot of words one can develop an intuitive feeling about word-stress. However, not everyone will be able to devise their own conscious or subconscious rules from large amounts of data. The obvious alternative is, therefore, to present the rules. In view of the fact that full descriptions of English word-stress tend to be book-sized (Fudge 1984; Poldauf 1984), there is a need to highlight the essentials.

▶ TASK 80

Look at the excerpt overleaf from Ponsonby (1987).

How useful do you find these rules? How many words will they cover in an average text? What is their relationship with the practice section? What special problem arises with the examples in A(e)?

A few general rules

(a) Always stress the syllable *before* one that's pronounced [ʃn] -ssion/-tion, [ʃs] -cious/ -tious, [ʃl] -cial/-tial, etc., e.g. atténtion, spácious, artifícial.

(b) In words ending '-ic', '-ical', '-ically', the stress is on the syllable *before* '-ic', *except* Árabic, aríthmetic, lúnatic, héretic, pólitics, rhétoric (*but* adjectives: arithmétic, herétical, polítical, rhetórical).

(c) A great many words are stressed on the last syllable but two, e.g. illúminate, thermómeter, geólogy, philósopher. Words ending in '-ólogy', '-ónomy', '-ósophy', 'ólogist', etc., always follow this rule.

(d Words ending in '-ese' have the stress on this syllable (Chinése, journalése).

(e) Do not stress the negative prefix attached to an adjective (póssible, impóssible; líterate, illíterate) *except*: nówhere, nóthing, nóbody, nónsense.

PRACTICE

A. *Exaggerate the stressing as much as you can—i.e. make the stressed syllable louder, higher and longer than the unstressed ones.*

(a) completion efficient invasion financial advantageous vivacious

(b) photogenic scientific materialistic geographical musical technical

(c) psychology/psychologist meteorology/meteorologist ideology/ideologist

(d) Chinese Japanese Portuguese Cantonese Balinese Viennese

(e) organised/disorganised complete/incomplete attractive/unattractive legal/illegal where/nowhere sense/nonsense

(Ponsonby 1987: 14)

These specifications do not, in fact, include a general rule covering the vast majority of English words, but pick out a number of suffixes which condition stress placement in polysyllabic words. There is no clear indication, for instance, that word-class membership is an important factor (the 'exceptions' in (b), for instance, can be explained by that). The special problem with the negative prefixes in A(e) is that in the context of the exercise they invite the use of contrastive stress on the negative prefix, thus contradicting the rule they are meant to illustrate.

The following extract from Rogerson and Gilbert (1990) shows how a set of clear headings helps to avoid the proliferation of confusing detail.

▶ **TASK 81**

In what respect is this set of rules more general than the first one? Would you present it to your students before or after work with actual data?

Summary

Word stress rules

1 *Stress on first syllable*
   Most two-syllable nouns and adjectives have stress on the first syllable:
   e.g. BUTter   PRETty

2 *Stress on last syllable*
   Most two-syllable verbs have stress on the last syllable:
   e.g. beGIN   proDUCE

3 *Stress on penultimate syllable* (second from the end)
   Words ending in 'ic':
   e.g. STAtic   reaLIStic
   Words ending in 'sion' and 'tion':
   e.g. teleVIsion   soLUtion

4 *Stress on ante-penultimate syllable* (third from the end)
   Words ending in 'cy', 'ty', 'phy', 'gy':
   e.g. deMOcracy   reliaBIlity
   Words ending in 'al':
   e.g. CRItical   ecoNOmical

5 *'Polysyllabic' words* (words with many syllables)
   These usually have more than one stress, i.e. a 'primary' and 'secondary' stress:
   e.g. interNAtional antibiotic
   Often such words contain a prefix (as with 'inter' and 'anti' above) and this prefix has a secondary stress (this is common with many long technical words).

6 *'Compound' words* (words with two parts)
   If the compound is a noun, the stress goes on the first part:
   e.g. GREENhouse   BLACKbird
   If the compound is an adjective, the stress goes on the second part:
   e.g. bad-TEMpered   old-FASHioned
   If the compound is a verb, the stress goes on the second part:
   e.g. underSTAND   overLOOK

(Rogerson and Gilbert 1990: 23)

The second question in Task 81 is of more general concern: we favoured discovery and perception before, and in connection with English word-stress the case is a particularly strong one. Lists of rules, even if they are set out clearly, are usually hard to remember and even harder to apply spontaneously. Letting the learners discover rules themselves greatly enhances the chance that they will actually remember them. The danger with this approach, however, is that the generalizations made by the learners may well be different from what was intended, thus calling for careful guidance on part of the teacher.

▶ TASK 82

Here are two of Rogerson and Gilbert's discovery exercises and one from *Headway Pronunciation*. What rules can you deduce? Learners with a strongly analytic mind could find the third activity confusing. Why?

B

Listen and then repeat these words (they are all nouns).

ENglish	staTIStics	inforMAtion
SCIence	comPUter	regisTRAtion
PHYsics	reACtion	
LANguage	linGUIstics	

Can you see a pattern?

C

Listen and mark the stress placement in these words.

calculation	decision	reaction
solution	distribution	television
relation	association	operation

What is the pattern? Can you define a 'rule'?

(Rogerson and Gilbert 1990: 20)

● **Word focus**

Do this exercise after the questionnaire on pages 22–3 of the Student's Book

3 Words ending in *-ion*

1 Most of the words below come from the job questionnaire in the Student's Book. Can you remember what they all mean?

Before you listen, try to guess where the stress is in each of these words.

profession	promotion	instruction
fashion	conclusion	occupation
question	completion	emotion
solution	option	communication

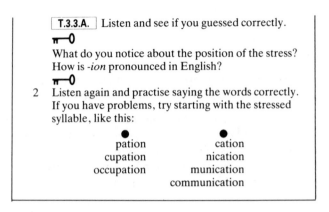

(Bowler and Cunningham 1991: 16)

On the basis of the data in B, we could say that English nouns are stressed on the penultimate syllable, a rule which does not occur in Rogerson and Gilbert's rules summary. The activity from *Headway* may cause confusion because *-ion* is not really a morpheme; *-ation* is a suffix, but what about *-ion* in 'fashion', 'question', and 'emotion'?

The need to work on word-stress may vary enormously from language to language. In the case of English it is not always easy to find a middle ground between representing the state of affairs as 'chaotic' and devising the vast number of rules necessary to achieve a consistent description. In many situations, the decision to do mostly without explicit rules and focus on stressed-syllable identification may be the best choice.

Another important point about word-stress activities is that they practically always work with words in isolation. Words are treated as utterances by themselves, which is not how they usually appear in natural language. In **8.3** we will look at the role which the overall rhythm of connected speech plays in the distribution of stresses in longer utterances. In **8.4** we will take a look at the opposite side of the coin, and consider questions of unstress.

8.3 The mystery of stress-time

We argued in **4.4** that a theory which neatly distinguishes between stress-timed and syllable-timed languages is overstated. Stress-time has, however, left its trace in numerous ELT coursebooks. Faber explains this in the following way:

'[the theory of stress-time] has received widespread and uncritical acceptance from those involved in TEFL, and this is not surprising. The theory is, in appearance at least, conveniently simple, it seems to explain why so many foreign learners get English speech-rhythm wrong (such learners are supposedly speakers of syllable-timed languages, while

English is stress-timed), and until recently this has been the only theoretical model available.'
(Faber 1986: 207)

In this unit we will look at some of the methodological consequences of focusing on stress-time and at some possible alternatives.

Within the theory of stress-time, the first and foremost principle to get across to the second language learner is that in English stress-beats occur at regular time-intervals. This is usually done by devising some acoustic or visual signal symbolizing the 'higher order' regular beat. The use of a metronome is perhaps the most striking way of establishing this regular tick-tock.

▶ **TASK 83**

If you have access to a metronome, or an electronic keyboard with a rhythm beat, try reading the following (or any other nursery rhyme, or a limerick) several times, increasing the speed with every reading.

> Jack Sprat could eat no fat
> His wife could eat no lean.
> And so between them both, you see,
> They licked the platter clean.
> Jack ate all the lean,
> His wife ate all the fat,
> The bone they picked it clean,
> Then gave it to the cat.

While this may be a good method to improve speech rate and articulatory dexterity, it is hardly fair to expect non-native speakers to do something that natives can only achieve with considerable effort. Rapping, for instance, is a display of articulatory dexterity that not every native speaker can manage.

Few teaching materials suggest actually using a metronome, but try to transport the importance of isochrony in some other way. Teachers and learners are often advised to tap on desks, clap their hands, or make conducting movements. In the next Task you will find two typical activities of this kind.

► TASK 84

Do the exercises below. Notice how the layout of the page conveys the regularity of the stress beats. How successful are you?

B i r d s	**e a t**	**w o r m s.**
The **b i r d s**	**e a t**	**w o r m s.**
The **b i r d s**	**e a t**	the **w o r m s.**
The **b i r d s**	will **e a t**	the **w o r m s.**
The **b i r d s**	willhave **e a t**en	the **w o r m s.**

'Use your index finger to tap out a regular rhythm on the edge of a table, keeping the beats constant, at about one beat per second. Say the sentences above, so that the three stresses in each sentence coincide with a tap.'
(Avery and Ehrlich 1992: 74)

B. *Here are three groups of numbers of different lengths on the paper, but which should take the same amount of time to say:*

(a)

twó	thrée	foúr
twénty	thírty	fórty
twó hundred	thrée hundred	foúr hundred

(b) *three groups of words of similar difficulty:*

a	níce	rípe	péar
a	lóve-ly	júicy	mélon
a de-	lí-cious and	móuth-wat(e)ring	píneapple

(Ponsonby 1987: 30)

It is rather difficult to utter the bottom lines in the same time as the first; at the very least our speech style changes from slow and deliberate in the first line to rapid conversational in the second.

When we listen to natural, spontaneous speech, it is not always easy to believe in the existence of a regular beat. Rhymes, poems, and limericks, on the other hand, provide a kind of positive 'evidence' for a strong 'pre-existing' rhythm. It is therefore not surprising that they figure prominently in practice materials under the heading 'stress-timed rhythm'.

▶ ## TASK 85

How do you feel about the following arguments for including extensive (humorous) rhythmical material in a pronunciation practice book?

'... the humourous line or nonsense verse lends itself, in practice, to an artificial range of tone and exaggerated stress. The material is ridiculous, therefore the manner of speech can likewise be ridiculous. When extremes are mastered, it has been found that speech and reading ... become much more vital and interesting as a result.'
(Barnard 1959)

In our experience, students do enjoy the verses a great deal, but regard them as a type of 'fun' information on English popular culture. At the same time, they tend to be very sceptical that this might have something to do with the rhythms of natural, spontaneous speech. The regularity of speech rhythms may vary a lot according to text type or speech style, but also individual habit.

'The stressed syllables and their accompanying muscular movements elsewhere in the body will tend to occur at roughly equal intervals of time but just as in any other human activities, swimming for instance, some beats will be slightly early, some slightly late and some may be missing altogether. The more organized the speech the more rhythmical it will be.'
(Brown 1990: 44)

In quite a number of recent teaching materials, the focus has shifted away from the isochrony principle towards differentiation between stressed and unstressed syllables. In fact, the word 'rhythm' tends to be used rather sparingly. Rhythm is seen as a by-product of the alternation of weak and strong syllables, rather than something which exists independently and in its own right.

▶ ## TASK 86

The following activities revolve around the perception of stress and unstress.

What is the focus in each? Why should we spend time on perception?

A

You will hear twelve sentences. Do you hear a series of stressed syllables or is the sentence made of syllables of different lengths? Make two columns under the following headings, with the numbers 1 to 12. As you listen, put a cross in the appropriate column.

Regular syllable length   *Irregular syllable length*
(all stressed syllables)   (stressed and unstressed syllables)

(Rogerson and Gilbert 1990: 25)

B

Listen and then underline the content words in the following sentences.

1 Can I have a coffee and a cup of tea, please?
2 Would you like another one?
3 Thanks for a lovely meal.
4 Sorry but I can't come on Monday because I'm working late.
5 I've never been to a car rally.
6 I usually visit my parents on Tuesdays.

(Rogerson and Gilbert 1990: 29)

4   How many stresses? Where are they?
Listen to the recording to check your answers.

I wondered if you were free on Tuesday. (3)
In the afternoon?
I'd like you to meet her.
I'm trying to fix the Directors' meeting.
Can you tell me what days you're free . . .
Friday's a bit difficult.
I'd like to make an appointment . . .
There's a lot to talk about.
It'll take a couple of hours . . .
I'll call you back in about half an hour . . .
I'm playing tennis until a quarter past.

(Swan and Walter 1985: 29)

The general principle 'perception before production' is valid here, too, but there is also a more direct benefit for the language learner. Coping with strings of slurred and unidentifiable (weak) syllables is essential for understanding natural, native-speaker utterances. In these tasks learners practise predicting stresses. Knowing that one can usually get by with merely picking up the words which are stressed can greatly enhance learners' listening success.

Summary
In this section we have seen that different theories about speech rhythm result in a preference for different activity types. What may be somewhat surprising is that subscribers to the theory of stress-time hardly ever include activities for the *perception* of the 'strong, regular beat' supposedly existing in the English language. All is geared towards the production of the regular rhythm. Teaching materials based on the more recent strong–weak syllable approach, on the other hand, focus on training learners to perceive the alternation of strong and weak syllables in order to heighten their awareness of speech rhythms. They use a bottom-up approach in this respect. It cannot be denied, however, that the top-down 'universal tick-tock' of stress-time still represents an appealingly neat categorization, so that references to stress-time (especially with regard to English) are still frequent.

8.4 Unstress and weak forms

As non-native speakers of English tend to have too many stresses in their speech, it seems that not only stress but also unstress needs explicit attention in the English language classroom. In English pronunciation coursebooks there exists a tradition of teaching unstress in the guise of *weak forms*. Mortimer states that 'a good practical grasp of the weak forms of English is essential to good pronunciation and listening comprehension' (Mortimer 1985: 4).

What are weak forms? As mentioned in 5.3, the main carriers of meaning, which tend to carry the stresses, are usually nouns, verbs, adjectives, adverbs of time, place, and manner, and demonstratives. Another class of words (articles, prepositions, pronouns, and conjunctions) mainly serves to express grammatical relationships. These have been called function words. Since function words are usually unstressed in utterances, their 'normal form' is the one containing a weak vowel, the weak form.

A common way of going about teaching weak forms is to have a section in the coursebook where weak forms are presented in lists and practised in a certain amount of context.

▶ TASK 87

The following two extracts are examples of this approach. What could be the advantage of having a list of weak forms? What about other weak forms in the two extracts?

Extract 1

	A. *Weak forms (shwa)*	B. *Strong forms (full value)*
a. an [ə] [ən]	I swallowed a fly. An alligator bit him.	You say *a* book, *a* child but *an* apple, *an* elephant.
am [əm] ['m]	What am I doing? I'm singing a song.	What *am* I to do? *Am* I serious? Yes, I'm afraid I *am*!
and [ən] ['n] [ənd]	Bread an(d) butter. Over an(d) over an(d) over again.	Trifle or jelly? Trifle *and* jelly, please! *And* she's a gossip . . .
are [ə] [ər]	Where are my glasses? Her cakes are awful!	They *are* mine, they *are*, they *are*! *Are* you alone?

(Ponsonby 1987: 64)

Extract 2 (the relevant weak form is in light type)

> 1 a /ə/
> A: So what went wrong?
> B: Well you said all I needed was a pencil, a ruler, a piece of wood, a saw, a hammer and a couple of nails.
> A: I said you needed a pencil, a ruler ... and a bit of common sense.

(Mortimer 1985: 5)

Mortimer, in fact, acknowledges that there may be 'words not in light type which need to be pronounced weakly if the dialogue is to be spoken properly' (1985: 4). In this particular dialogue these are 'you', 'was', 'of', 'and', but he recommends that 'primary attention should be given to the weak forms actually specified in the heading'. The problem with this strategy is that one weak form is picked out while the others are typographically lumped together with the stressed content words. However, the difficulty of how to represent weak forms typographically is really only a symptom of something else: namely the fact that 'paying attention to weak forms' leaves teachers and learners in a paradoxical situation. Weak forms are weak precisely because speakers pass over them quickly. So in 'concentrating on them' we are actually trying hard not to pay attention to them—something which requires considerable mental acrobatics.

There is another 'psychological barrier' to reducing weak syllables which might be even more serious for the language learner.

▶   # TASK 88

Avery and Ehrlich (1992: 65–6) give the following advice:

'It is extremely important for both you and your students to recognize the pronouncing unstressed vowels as schwa is not lazy or sloppy. All native speakers of Standard English (including the Queen of England, The Prime Minister of Canada, and the President of the United States) use schwa.'

What do you think is their motivation for this explicit advice? What aspects of learner speech tend to prevent the production of 'properly (un)stressed' utterances?

Kenworthy pinpoints the problem (and a possible solution) in the following way:

'Every word seems important to someone who is struggling to put together a message in a new language. Indeed the concern 'not to leave anything out' often leads to overstressing; ... We need activities which make learners think about the relative importance of parts of a message.'
(Kenworthy 1987: 33)

The classic awareness exercise in this respect revolves around sending telegrams (as they contain only content words and everything that can be left out is a function word or weak form).

C

Look at these telex messages and see if you can expand them into complete sentences.
Example: SEND PARCEL AIRMAIL.
            'Could you send the parcel by airmail?'

(There is more than one possible version in most cases.)
1 CONFIRM ARRIVAL ORDER NO 235/SA.
2 PLEASE CONTACT. URGENT MESSAGE.
3 REGRET DELAY DUE FERRY STRIKE.
4 ARRIVING MILAN AIRPORT TUES 09.00.
5 CONFERENCE POSTPONED. CANCEL FLIGHTS.

(Rogerson and Gilbert 1990: 29)

▶   TASK 89

Some of the rhythm exercises we have looked at might also be recycled for the purpose of building awareness about weak forms. Look at the activities presented in Task 86. How could you turn them into activities on weak forms? Is there an advantage to using material for more than one purpose?

If students are asked to name the kinds of words which are stressed and the kinds of words which are not, they do not usually find it hard to come up with a list of relevant word-classes. This may remind you (or your students) of work done on prominence (see 5.3 and 7.3). The motivation for recycling material in this fashion is that 'sentence stress' and weak forms are as inseparable as the two sides of a coin. Treating them under separate headings in separate sections of a coursebook may result in students missing the point.

In this unit we have seen that treating weak forms as something special and separate may not be the ideal way of getting across how essential they are for the 'right sound' of spoken English. It is important to realize that weak forms are a logical consequence of how this language treats unstressed syllables. Weak forms are thus just another aspect of connected speech. In the next sub-section we shall look at some more.

9 Focus on connected speech

We saw in 3 how the connected speech processes of assimilation, elision, and linking alter the sound of words and make them differ from the 'ideal' shape they have when pronounced in isolation. The resulting reduction of phonetic information about words and word-boundaries is probably responsible for the widespread feeling among foreign language learners that the natives of any language 'speak too fast'.

9.1 Teaching for perception or teaching for production?

What can we do as teachers to help our students cope with natural spoken language? There is, of course, always the option of letting the situation take care of itself: once learners have built up a stock of second language expectations through plenty of language exposure and experience, they will be able to cope with acoustic underspecification and may even introduce modified forms into their own speech. Most teaching materials, however, seem to favour a more positive course of action and include activities on connected speech phenomena. The extent of these activities ranges from regular units entitled 'Connected speech' (for example, in the *Headway Pronunciation* series) to occasional hints included in comments on reading exercises (for example, Barnard 1959).

There is, however, considerable difference of opinion about *why* connected speech should be taught. For example:

'If speakers avoid all assimilations (even when speaking slowly), they will sound very formal.'
(Gimson and Ramsaran 1982: 62)

'[connected speech] helps explain why written English is so different from spoken English.'
(Rogerson and Gilbert 1990: 31)

'Extensive work on the aspects of connected speech ... will not only contribute to students' ability to produce fluent and comprehensible speech, but also to their ability to comprehend the spoken language.'
(Avery and Ehrlich 1992: 89)

'Connected Speech: these exercises look at the way that the pronunciation of individual words can change when they are part of a phrase or a sentence.'
(Bowler and Cunningham 1990: viii)

According to Ponsonby (1987: 44, 88), linking and elision are 'aids that help us to maintain the fluency of the rhythm'.

▶ ## TASK 90

Consider the above statements. Which reason(s) do you find most important?

The fact that knowing about connected speech phenomena facilitates *listening* is probably uncontroversial, but several of the quotations also make reference to *production*. How far the teaching of connected speech should aim at production on the part of the foreign learner is much more open to debate, though.

▶ ## TASK 91

The following two extracts formulate alternative positions on this issue. Which do *you* find more convincing?

'At first, many students have to be convinced that it is "correct" to use these expressions. However, as they begin to practise them, they notice their use in spoken language and realize their importance for comprehensibility.'
(Naiman 1992: 168)

'I have already suggested that I do not approve of teaching students to *produce* 'assimilated' forms and elided forms. Sophisticated students who have been taught to be aware of these forms will introduce them into their own speech in a natural context when they feel able to control them'.
(Brown 1990: 158)

Naiman seems to favour active use of connected speech forms by language learners. Brown (1990: 62–5) argues that learner speech seldom meets the conditions for connected speech phenomena to occur naturally. In native speech, assimilation, elision, and linking occur because it tends to be fluent and rapid and contains many obscured syllables. Both these aspects tend to be under-represented in the speech of second language learners, so that the sudden occurrence of a few (painstakingly practised) assimilated forms would be incongruent with their overall speech style.

In an attempt to reconcile these opposing views, we might consider differentiating between types of connected speech phenomena with regard to their importance for the second language learner. Roach has suggested the following:

'It would not be practical or useful to teach all learners of English to produce assimilations; practice in making elisions is more useful, and it is clearly valuable to do exercises related to ... linking.'
(Roach 1991: 130)

Roach also stresses the importance of work on connected speech for listening. The most serious problem second language learners have in this area are the comprehension problems caused by the blurring of word-boundaries. What seems to be called for here is to make learners aware of what is going on and to help them build up the right expectations about the kind of sound patterns they are likely to be confronted with in normal native speech.

It will always be the teacher's decision to judge the relative benefits of the effort necessary to acquire active or even native-like competence in connected speech. In our experience, simplifications which occur inside words often go unnoticed and hardly ever cause trouble because the middle of a word is not as prominent as its beginning. Take, for example, elision in [krɪsməs], where the fact that there is no /t/ in 'Christmas' will not even reach consciousness level. In those cases, however, where the learners' first language exhibits the same simplification strategies as the second language, we have found that learners can profit greatly from having their attention drawn to what exactly is happening on the sound level. In the first language, natural fluency is a matter of course and connected speech phenomena are regarded as 'sloppiness' only in extremely formal styles when the level of self-consciousness is high. In the second language our self-consciousness tends to be high at all times. But once learners know that simplifications are normal, once they possess declarative knowledge about connected speech phenomena, they are often able to convert this knowledge into active, procedural knowledge with astounding ease. In 9.2 we will look more closely at how the three connected speech phenomena of assimilation, elision, and linking are treated in coursebooks.

9.2 Assimilation, elision, and linking

Assimilation
It is noticeable that American pronunciation materials tend to have more extended coverage of assimilation than materials based on British pronunciation. The reason for this might be that assimilation features are more frequent in American English than in British English; certainly they are more prominent psychologically, as is witnessed by the existence of alternative spellings (for example, 'gotcha', 'wanna'). Perhaps it is this that makes for the strong feeling on part of teachers of American pronunciation that learners should be made aware of them.

The assimilation phenomenon exemplified in 'gotcha' is palatalization: the fact that before a [j]-sound [t] turns into [tʃ], [d] turns into [dʒ], [s] turns into [ʃ], and [z] into [ʒ]. Such sequences often occur when a verb, an auxiliary, a question word, or a negative particle is followed by 'you' or 'yet' (for example, 'can't you', 'should you', 'where did you', 'when's your date', 'won't you', 'not yet', etc.). Phrases such as these are extremely common in everyday colloquial speech, and a semi-official alternative spelling has established itself in American English: 'cantcha', 'wheredja', 'wontcha', 'wouldja', etc. Morley (1992: 42) includes an extensive list of such combinations. Hagen and Grogan propose the following activity for practising these assimilations in context:

Exercise 11: Interview

Part A: Interview a student in the class and a native speaker of English. Write their answers in the blanks, and remember to have them sign their names. Use the reductions studied in this chapter (some of the more difficult ones are given to you in parentheses). Study each question before you speak so that you do not have to read it. You may want to practice with a partner first.

1. What did you (*whajya*) do yesterday?
2. What do you (*whachya*) do every day?
3. How did you (*howja*) get your first job?
4. When's your next vacation?
5. Where did you (*whereja*) go on your last vacation?
6. What can't you do?
7. What shouldn't you do?
8. Why did you agree to this interview?

Answers:

1.　　　　　　　　　　　1.

2.　　　　　　　　　　　2.

(Hagen and Grogan 1992: 168)

In this particular case, the use of a question and answer game suggests itself quite naturally, as questions are by far the most frequent syntactic environment in which these assimilations occur. Very often, though, such natural contexts are not at hand.

▶ **TASK 92**

Consider the following extract from an assimilation awareness activity. What problems might there be?

1 Give each learner a copy of this worksheet containing the following (example) questions:

In rapid speech:
1 When is a /n/ a /m/?
2 When is a /t/ a /p/?
3 When is a /d/ a /b/?
4 When is a /s/ a /ʃ/?
5 When is a /z/ a /ʒ/?
6 When is a /n/ a /ŋ/?
7 When is a /d/ a /g/?
8 When is a /t/ a /k/?

© Longman Group UK Ltd 1992

2 Give each learner a jumbled list of examples where such assimilations take place.

Examples

ten green bottles	she was born in
ten pin bowling	Birmingham
she has, has she?	the right key
this shirt	white paper
good boy	ten players
good girl	bit part
good morning	speed boat

© Longman Group UK Ltd 1992

(Bowen and Marks 1992: 51)

The purpose of the short phrases in the above extract is to serve as material for *analysis* on the part of the learners. As soon as active production comes into play, we need to be aware that short, isolated items do not actually invite the type of articulation which gives rise to connected speech phenomena.

Elision

In **3.2** we mentioned that elision (the deletion of sounds in connected speech) mostly affects the English sounds /h/, /t/, /d/, and schwa, so that the number of changes that need to be learnt is limited. Nevertheless, Temperley (1987) reports that awareness among EFL students of this way of linking words together is very low. In a survey among advanced students of English, she found that only one-fifth had ever heard of consonant deletion. She continues:

'Some teachers might say that a learner's transitions between words become more native as fluency develops, or that the lack of these transitions results in nothing worse than a foreign accent. However, we know

that a learner can develop fluency without achieving an acceptable level of intelligible pronunciation. Words become linked, but in a non-English way.'
(Temperley 1987: 66)

One such example of non-English deletion is mentioned by Kenworthy (1987: 140): Greek speakers tend to 'simplify' final *nd*, *mb*, and *ng* by dropping the nasal consonant, so that 'bend' becomes 'bed', and 'send' may be misheard as 'said'.

▶ **TASK 93**

Do you know of any other such non-English simplifications?

Do your own students use any?

German speakers, for instance, often over-generalize the deletion of schwa in final syllables, which is suspended in many British placenames ending in *-don*. For 'Swindon', for instance, they say [swɪndn] instead of [swɪndən].

It may be a good idea to get students interested in sound deletions by using examples where deletion makes their life easier. Plural forms like 'clothes' and 'months', or phrases like 'first thing' are hard to articulate and learners are grateful to hear that even the natives have developed ways to get round such difficult combinations, for example by dropping the /ð/ in 'clothes' and the final /t/ in 'first', or by turning the /θ/ in 'months' into a /t/.

If one wants to go on to some more systematic teaching after such anecdotal awareness raising, it is often difficult to find the relevant sections in coursebooks. In many teaching materials, the different manifestations of the same basic processes are treated under several different headings: elision, sound deletion, simplification, reduction, contraction, and also linking.

The dropping of /h/ in unstressed pronouns ('his', 'her', 'him', 'he'), for instance, is often called 'reduction' (for example, Rogerson and Gilbert 1990: 33; Hagen and Grogan 1992: 99). Hagen and Grogan also include the dropping of /h/ in auxiliary 'have' ('could have been', etc.), something which elsewhere comes under the heading of 'contractions', together with 'will', 'is', 'are', etc. ('I'll', 'she's', 'we're').

But apart from questions of terminology, it is also important to point out that the use of elided and unelided forms depends on the choice of speech style.

▶ TASK 94

What kinds of stylistic differences can be pointed out by teaching contractions?

At what level(s) of proficiency would you find teaching contractions useful?

Contractions can serve to introduce learners to the differences between spoken and informal written language on the one hand, and formal written language on the other. As contractions affect very basic structures, learners need to know them early on. Usually, they are also taught early on, mostly by juxtaposing full forms with contracted forms and ascribing them different stylistic values (formal/informal), the two forms standing side by side like two different vocabulary items; for example, 'that is'–'that's', 'I cannot'–'I can't'. What is missing most of the time is an explanation as to why the two different forms look the way they do.

▶ TASK 95

Can you think of a simple explanation which could be given to near-beginners?

Rogerson and Gilbert use the following phrasing: 'Contractions are used to de-emphasise the less important words. This helps to highlight the more important words.' (1990: 34). The phrasing of this explanation has an important advantage: it allows the teacher (and the learner) to relate the chapter 'contractions' to much more general principles of connected speech such as prominence, stress, and the obscuring of unstressed syllables.

As with assimilation, teachers trying to present elision face the problem of having to bridge the gap between the short phrases used for analysis ('What happens to the last consonant of the first word?') and the larger contexts which are necessary for production.

▶ TASK 96

Consider the following extract. How well do the contexts work? How might one go about devising an activity which shows elision in the kind of environment where it occurs in natural speech?

Linking Words and Holding Plosive Sounds
Practice each of the sentences in Group C. Then write an additional sentence for the pair of linked words. Practice these sentences. Audio or video record them.

Group C

1. We took : Kay to the game.   _____

2. I need : time to finish my homework.   _____

3. Don't : tell the teacher I was late.   _____

4. I must help : Bob with his homework.   _____

5. We didn't : take the bus.   _____

Practice the pairs of linked words in Group D. Write sentences for each pair. Practice your sentences and audio or video record them.

Group D

1. _____ next : Tuesday _____ .   _____

2. _____ back : tire _____ .   _____

3. _____ next : time _____ .   _____

4. _____ look : tired _____ .   _____

(Morley 1992: 44)

If we want the speech rate to be as natural as possible, the obvious choice is to start out with a full listening text. From there, we can pick out those instances where elision actually happens. In principle, any listening text will do, but radio news broadcasts, with their emphasis on 'correct speech', will serve the purpose particularly well. The following exercise on elision is constructed along the lines suggested here: after the learners have worked on the contents of the news broadcasts, they are confronted with the task overleaf.

---

5 **Pronunciation. You will hear some extracts from the news broadcasts. Listen particularly to the phrases below. Notice how the ends of the words are pronounced, and how one word is joined to the next. Then say the phrases yourselves.**

government proposals
wanted Switzerland to become
preferred to keep
have smashed their way
best known for his song
left by the raiders
he's had to halt work
last night
flames swept through a garage
a dustbin was hurled through the front window
police were called to the scene
a cloudy start to the day
sunshine in most parts
top temperatures
rain and drizzle

(Swan and Walter 1987: 53)

▶   TASK 97

Which rules can you deduce from the data provided in the activity? Do you think the activity should be accompanied by explicit rules?

The phrases in the activity and their realization by the newsreaders give ample evidence of the deletion of /t/ and /d/ between two other consonants, both within words and across word-boundaries. There are also examples of incomplete release of the first of two identical consonants ('flames swept', 'start to'), and advanced students do not find it too difficult to formulate their own rules.

Linking

We have already noticed that the lack of a consistent terminology makes it difficult to compare the treatment of connected speech in coursebooks. The term *linking*, in particular, is used in two different ways. Quite often it is synonymous with what we have called *connected speech phenomena* in general because they all act together to create units larger than the single word. In this book, however (see **3.2**), we use a definition of linking which is more specific: *it applies only to what happens at word-boundaries where either two vowels or a consonant and a vowel meet.*

Consider word-boundaries involving a consonant and a vowel, for example 'get out'. In such a case the final consonant of the first word is treated as if it belonged to the following word ('ge-tout'). This is why this kind of linking has also been called *catenation*. In **3.2** we pointed out that this is often responsible for learners' confusion regarding the identification of word-boundaries.

'Some students have learned English through the eye rather than through the ear, resulting in the false notion that words should be pronounced the way they look on the printed page, each one separated by blank spaces. Their speech typically is replete with pauses, one after every word.'
(Wong 1987: 48–9)

We might add that these learners also expect to *hear* a pause after each word.

Apart from the need to practise catenation in order to ensure correct word-recognition, Wong points out that catenation activities may benefit students on another level, too. Many languages do not allow syllable-final consonants at all, so that, in general, final consonants and consonant clusters are hard to pronounce for speakers of such languages. Catenation causes the restructuring of syllables so that final clusters become initial, for example 'watch out' CVC+VC becomes 'wa+chout' CV+CVC. Linking phenomena can be seen as a trend towards overriding a language's more complex syllable structure towards the universally preferred CV sequence (Wong 1987: 49).

The trend towards creating CV sequences is perhaps even more visible/audible at word-boundaries where two vowels meet and the consonantal glides /j/, /w/, /r/ are inserted. British materials tend to include more work on these aspects of linking. Where they are neglected, even advanced learners are very insecure about how acceptable it is to use linking 'r's. In American English there is no need for 'r'-linking, as *postvocalic* /r/ is pronounced anyway; Hagen and Grogan (1992: 79), for instance, suggest leaving the perception of /j/- or /w/-linking to advanced students (and their good ear) and concentrate exclusively on catenation.

As we suggested for assimilation and elision, linking too is best demonstrated 'in action'. Any running text should do for this purpose. Some coursebooks introduce texts for reading out loud with the general instruction to 'pay attention to word-linking'. Alternatively, textbooks may include 'purpose-built' texts (usually dialogues) for students to detect and revise linking and connected speech phenomena at large.

▶ TASK 98

Compare the following extract to the extract from a natural conversation on pages 50–1. Try to find all instances of assimilation, elision, and linking in both texts, and mark them. How frequent are they in each text?

---

4 Word linking in informal speech – revision

1 | **T.12.4.** | If you listen to the dialogue at the beginning of Unit 12 in the Student's Book it is a rather **formal** conversation. But listen to a similar dialogue which is very *informal*:

Steve Hello this is Steve – can I speak to Alison please?

Paul I'm afraid she's having a shower at the moment – can she ring you back?

Steve Mmm . . . well, all right, but I'm going out in a couple of minutes. I'll be back in about two hours okay – can she phone me back then?

Paul I think she's going out later herself – oh hang on, she's just coming out of the shower – I'll pass you over to her okay . . .

Could you catch all the words? If not listen again until you can.

(Bowler and Cunningham 1990: 68)

Even though the textbook dialogue does not sound unnatural, it shows a higher concentration of what is being worked on, and is therefore useful for concentrated practice. Besides, there are fewer distractors in the shape of unknown vocabulary or names. Natural texts might then come in at a later stage for recycling and consolidation.

10 Focus on sounds

We have outlined (in **2.1** and **2.2**) what seems to be, according to a fairly broad consensus, the minimum knowledge which foreign language teachers need to have of phonetics and phonology with respect to the articulation and function of speech sounds. It is important to bear in mind, though, that when we talk about these sound *segments* we refer to idealizations of the sounds which occur in connected speech, embedded in and dependent on situational and contextual factors which are reflected more directly in *suprasegmental* aspects such as stress, rhythm, and intonation.

In the same way that we use idealization as a descriptive convenience in order to be able to set up categories of sounds, so it may be useful in the teaching of these sounds to 'idealize them out' from the complexities of connected speech as a pedagogic strategy. This is what is done in activities teaching 'individual sounds'.

These individual sounds are much easier to describe in isolation than intonation and connected speech phenomena. Indeed, there is an abundance of materials available for teaching the sounds of particular languages, especially English, and what we emphatically do not want to do here is attempt an exhaustive coverage of these materials. Instead, we should like to select specific activities from textbooks and use them as prompts for addressing a few questions of principle about the teaching of speech sounds.

10.1 Ear training and awareness building

Most handbooks on pronunciation teaching emphasize the importance of ear training. MacCarthy (1978) maintains that many pronunciation problems experienced by learners are due to the fact that:

'the capacity of the ordinary person to perceive auditorily the phenomena of the language to be learnt is widely, but quite wrongly, taken for granted.'
(MacCarthy 1978: 14)

It is important to remember, therefore, that before learners can be asked to produce the sounds of a new language, they need to learn to perceive them, which means 'paying attention to them and noticing things about them' (MacCarthy 1978: 15).

▶ TASK 99
Consider the following examples of perceptual training tasks.
What is it that learners are being asked to perceive?

28   The yes/no game

Level   Beginner to advanced

Students   All ages, especially young learners

Groups   Whole class

Purpose   To improve discrimination of consonant sounds

Text type   Teacher's word list

In this activity

Students play an elimination game based on sound discrimination.

Preparation

Prepare a list of words containing consonants which cause difficulty for your
learners (see Appendix 8). The Sample teaching material below has been
chosen with Spanish speakers in mind, and involves contrasts between /n/ and
/ŋ/, /s/ and /θ/. For each student, make two cards, one marked YES and the
other marked NO. If you can make all the YES cards one colour and the NO
cards another, this will make things easier for you during the game.

Procedure

1. Give each learner a YES card and a NO card.

2. Explain that the learners will hear a list of words, some of which will
    contain a given sound. After each word, they must hold up one of their
    cards – YES if they think the word contains the given sound, and NO if not.
    If a learner holds up the wrong card, he/she is out of the game, and so is the
    last learner to raise a card.

3. Begin the game. It need not be based on one target sound alone, but on
    several, as in the sample. The game ends when only one learner is left in.

Sample teaching material

Word list: singer   rang   ran   thing   thin   sin
Teacher instruction: Hold up a YES card if you think you hear /n/ (or
/θ/). Hold up your NO card if you don't hear the sound.

Teacher's diary

Was there any evidence that this activity improved your learners'
ability to discriminate? Which sound(s) caused most problems?

(Taylor 1993: 87)

3.11

SOUNDS DISCRIMINATION EXERCISE

LEVEL
Beginner +

FOCUS
Recognising
minimal
differences
between
individual
phonemes

MATERIALS
A minimal pairs
worksheet (see
Example tasks
below)

TIME
10–20 minutes

This activity can help to sensitise learners to minimal differences between individual phonemes and enable them to recognise sounds in context. It can be regarded as an initial stage in the process of learning to produce these sounds accurately. You can use it as a warmer or as a remedial slot dealing with a particular problem. It is also useful as a basic listening exercise in terms of aural training.

Procedure

1 Give each learner a copy of the worksheet and ensure that they understand you are going to read contrasting sounds or words aloud to the class and that they must decide which sound is being uttered each time and indicate this by ticking the appropriate column next to the number.
2 Read the sounds or words aloud, pausing for a short time between each one to give the learners time to make a decision.
3 Check what the learners have ticked. Repeat, if necessary, any items that are causing problems.

EXTENSION
An activation stage can follow. Depending on the level of the class, further examples can be done in small pairs or groups, with the learners taking it in turns to play the role of the teacher. That is, one learner reads out a list of sounds or words and the others tick the sounds that they hear. A valuable side-product of this stage may be that the learners will tick a sound that the speaker did not intend them to tick and will do this because of inaccurate pronunciation by the speaker. This often has the effect of focusing attention on the pronunciation of a particular sound.

Example tasks

Tick the sound you hear	Teacher reads
1 /iː/ /ɪ/	/iː/
2 /uː/ /ʊ/	/ʊ/
3 /ɜː/ /ə/	/ə/
4 /e/ /ʌ/	/ʌ/
5 /ʌ/ /æ/	/æ/
6 /ɒ/ /ɔː/	/ɒ/
7 /θ/ /ð/	/θ/
8 /eɪ/ /aɪ/	/eɪ/
9 /b/ /p/	/p/
10 /r/ /l/	/l/

© Longman Group UK Ltd 1992

Tick the word you hear			Teacher reads
1 work	walk	woke	walk
2 main	mine	moan	main
3 herd	hard	hurt	hurt
4 pole	Paul	pale	pole
5 fair	four	fear	fear

© Longman Group UK Ltd 1992

(Bowen and Marks 1992: 36, 37)

Unit 3   The short vowels /ɒ/, /ʊ/ and /ʌ/

1   Match the words in each group that contain the same vowel sound. One is done for you.

watch	good	just	push	blood	book
looks	stopped	got	lunch	not	long
shut	stuck	pull	cough	cook	cut

(Hewings 1993: 4)

The primary objective of these activities is to help learners perceive the differences between the significant sounds of English. The main obstacle to hearing foreign sounds properly is that, as in all learning, we can only interpret what is new and unfamiliar in terms of what we know already—that is to say, we will tend to hear the sounds of a new language through the filter of our first language (see **2.2**). It is therefore important for learners to acquire not just the articulation of the new sounds, but the system of phonemes, i.e. the relevant oppositions. Joanne Kenworthy has a helpful simile for this process of recategorization:

'The nature of the task is basically similar to that of the fruit sorter who has been used to sorting apples into three sizes, A, B, and C and suddenly has to begin to sort the same crop of apples into four sizes. Consequently, in sorting two apples which would both formerly have fitted into category C, one of them must now be put in category C and the other in the new category D. The process of adjustment can be a difficult one.'
(Kenworthy 1987: 45)

The teacher's role at this stage is crucial, since he or she can provide opportunities for an experience of the target-language sounds in whatever way makes them most easily noticeable to the learners.

▶   **TASK 100**

Consider the activities illustrated in Task 99 above. Which aspects of phonetics and phonology would you expect to be helpful to teachers in devising appropriate perceptual training tasks for their learners? You may want to consult subsection **2** in thinking about this question.

Generally speaking, teachers need an understanding of both how sounds are articulated (phonetics), and what the significant sounds are in the relevant languages (phonology). Your answers will partly depend on the language background of your students, and hence the differences between their first language and the target language. The perceptual training tasks illustrated so far aim at highlighting the differences in phonological knowledge. There are also awareness-building activities for which phonetic knowledge, either about articulation in general or about the articulatory peculiarities of the target language, is likely to be helpful. Some authors, such as MacCarthy, urge teachers to begin with familiarizing learners with general auditory and articulatory distinctions, irrespective of the specific target language. Catford (1987: 99) emphasizes that students have to be taught 'precisely what to do with their vocal organs'. Joanne Kenworthy, on the other hand, reminds us that 'receiving directions about what to do with the vocal organs is completely alien to people' (Kenworthy 1987: 69). Nevertheless, she concedes that there are some postures and movements which learners usually find relatively easy to recognize and control. These are:

- lip position: whether the lips are pursed (as in whistling) or spread (as in a smile) or wide apart (as when yawning)
- contact (or close proximity) between the tongue and teeth: whether the sides of the tongue are touching the upper back teeth (the molars) or whether the tip of the tongue is touching the top or bottom front teeth
- contact (or close proximity) between the tongue and the roof of the mouth: whether the tip of the tongue is touching a part of the roof of the mouth, or whether the back of the tongue is.
  (Kenworthy 1987: 69ff.)

When students have been familiarized with the basic distinctions, they can be asked to do more taxing tasks which involve the presentation of an utterance and the asking of questions about it. MacCarthy (1976) suggests the following:

Exercise: Listen to this: $- - \backslash - -$

Stimulus F. pala: bukilo

How many syllables were there?	Answer: 5
How many different vowels?	Answer: 4
How many different consonants?	Answer: 4
How many diphthongs?	Answer: none
Which syllable had a longer vowel?	Answer: the second
Which syllable had falling pitch?	Answer: the third

(MacCarthy 1976: 306)

10.2 The fundamental problem: communicating vs. noticing

Insights arising from both descriptions of language use and research into conditions for successful second language acquisition have led to the claim that language teaching should be communicative, i.e. based on meaningful interaction rather than on the practice of isolated forms. On the other hand, this 'communicative claim' creates a problem for language pedagogy: in order for language items to be learnt, they need to be 'noticed' first (Schmidt 1990). And in order to be noticed, they need to be highlighted—learners need to be exposed to the forms they are to acquire. When it comes to the teaching and learning of the sounds of the target language, then, this means that the problem is how to make sure that these sounds occur in a sufficient concentration to be noticed while at the same time avoiding meaningless drills.

▶ TASK 101

Adrian Doff's book *Teach English: A Training Course for Teachers* (1988) contains a unit on teaching pronunciation. One activity asks readers to say which of the following steps are most important, and which are unnecessary, when focusing on sounds the students find difficult.

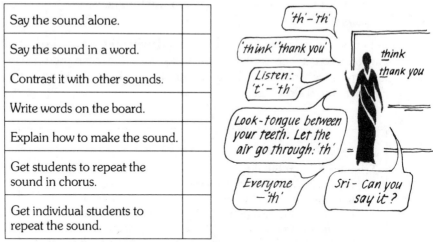

Say the sound alone.	
Say the sound in a word.	
Contrast it with other sounds.	
Write words on the board.	
Explain how to make the sound.	
Get students to repeat the sound in chorus.	
Get individual students to repeat the sound.	

(Doff 1988: 114)

Which of these steps might you want to avoid in a communicative classroom, and why?

Your reaction to the activities in this task will obviously depend on the specific teaching situation you are thinking of. What all of these steps do seem to highlight, though, is the difficulty of reconciling a narrow focus on particular sounds with the communicative objectives of learner involvement and meaningful interaction. As long ago as 1956, David Abercrombie warned that:

'no words or sentences ... should be introduced merely to illustrate points of pronunciation ... and the attainment of fluency should not be sacrificed to perfection of detail. The enthusiast might find himself, if he is not careful, with pupils who have a good pronunciation but nothing to pronounce.'
(Abercrombie 1956: 89)

The most common types of exercises for focusing on sound production are illustrated below. They are (a) listen and repeat, (b) minimal pairs, (c) minimal pair sentences, and (d) tongue twisters.

(a) Practice 1 Listen and repeat:

(Baker 1981: 4)

(b)

bead-bid	greased-grist	deal-dill	dean-din	he's-his
lead-lid	keyed-kid	meal-mill	lean-Lynn	breeches-britches
deed-did	steeple-stipple	real-rill	wean-win	eat-it
heed-hid	scheme-skim	seal-sill	sheen-shin	beat-bit
reed-rid	gene-gin	teal-till	keen-kin	heat-hit
greed-grid	ease-is	steal-still	green-grin	cheat-chit
leafed-lift	leave-live	eel-ill	seen-sin	wheat-whit
skied-skid	wheeze-whiz	feel-fill	teen-tin	meat-mitt
creeped-crypt	each-itch	heel-hill	heap-hip	neat-knit
ceased-cyst	beach-bitch	keel-kill	cheap-chip	peat-pit
leased-list	peach-pitch	kneel-nil	leap-lip	seat-sit
. . .				

(Nilsen and Nilsen 1971: 1)

(c) SENTENCES WITH CONTEXTUAL CLUES
Please SIT in this SEAT.
These shoes should FIT your FEET.
Do you STILL STEAL?
Those BINS are for BEANS.
They SHIP SHEEP.

MINIMAL SENTENCES
He lost the LEAD/LID.
This WEEK/WICK seems very long.
FEEL/FILL this bag.
She wore a NEAT/KNIT suit.
Don't SLEEP/SLIP on the deck.
(Nilsen and Nilsen 1971: 1)

(d) Peter Piper picked a peck of pickled peppers.

Did Peter Piper pick a peck of pickled peppers?

If Peter Piper picked a peck of pickled peppers

Where's the peck of pickled peppers Peter Piper picked?

(traditional, used in many textbooks)

Celce-Murcia calls these types of exercise 'techniques of the past which have never yielded very good results'. Her criticism of them is that:

'while useful on a limited, individual basis for purposes of correction and drill, none of these exercise types is in tune with the communicative approach to language teaching. The material they employ is artificial and unauthentic. With the focus on isolated words and/or sentences, there is little transfer from practice to natural communication. The structured and analytic nature of these drills also makes them extremely unmotivating.'
(Celce-Murcia 1987: 5)

▶ TASK 102

Do you agree with Celce-Murcia's criticism? Can you think of ways of embedding exercises such as the ones above in more meaningful interaction, so as to facilitate transfer to natural communication?

There are numerous ways in which drill-like activities can be modified to make them more meaningful for the learner while still retaining the focus on sounds, and most recent textbooks offer such variations. What they have in common is an endeavour to relate linguistic form to social meaning and action. This can be achieved through more active involvement on the part of the learners, a clearer specification of purpose, and a stronger element of choice—aspects which are in keeping with the factors of the speech event as discussed in 5.2. Joan Morley's three-volume course *Improving Spoken English: Consonants in Context* (1992) combines exercises with a 'microfocus' on pronunciation with a 'macrofocus' on spoken communication to achieve this integration.

▶ TASK 103

Extracts 1 and 2 are variations of minimal pair exercises. What advantages do you see in them over the traditional reading out of such pairs?

Extract 1

H _____

*Pair practice: sentences with **V** and **B***

Student 1 says sentence (a) or (b). Student 2 answers.

1. a He wants to buy my boat.	Will you sell it?
b. He wants to buy my vote.	That's against the law!
2. a. What's a bat?	A flying mouse.
b. What's a vat?	A container for liquid.
3. a. What does "vend" mean?	To sell.
b. What does "bend" mean?	To curve.

(*Gilbert 1993a: 20*)

Extract 2

TEST THE TEACHER

3.5

This is a variation on the use of minimal pairs which turns the tables and allows the learners to test the teacher. The same procedure can be applied to word stress patterns, intonation, rhythmic patterns in sentences. For this imaginary class, the contrasting sounds are /əʊ/ and /ɔː/, and the list might be:

oh	or
so	saw
low	law
coal	call
coat	caught
boat	bought

© Longman Group UK Ltd 1992

LEVEL
Any

FOCUS
Could be any aspect of pronunciation. This example is concerned with sound contrasts

MATERIALS
A list of minimal pairs containing sounds that your class confuse

Procedure

1 Write the list on the board as above.
2 Invite learners, one by one, to say any one of the words on the board. Say that you will point to the word you hear, and they should say 'Yes' if that was the word they said and 'No' if it wasn't.
3 Point silently to the word you hear, preferably with a pointer rather than your finger. If you aren't sure whether you have heard, for example, *coat* or *caught*, point in between the two. If you hear something different, like *curt* for instance, point somewhere else on the board.
4 If one of the learners says 'No' to your response, either give them more time straight away to try to refine their intended pronunciation, or let them wait a while until they are ready.

VARIATION
Instead of just a two-way sound contrast, you could use three or four confusing sounds for this activity.

RATIONALE
The learners are in control and the teacher gets the 'No' for being wrong, which makes it, at least for many learners, a fairly risk-free and enjoyable way of trying out the accuracy of their pronunciation.

(Bowen and Marks 1992: 31)

Michael Vaughan-Rees (1992: 49ff.) demonstrates that even tongue-twisters can be used creatively. His 'Do-it-yourself tongue-twister kit' allows learners to build their own alliterative sequences. This activity involves several steps, in one of which the students assign points to the sound combinations they have generated: for instance, 'Kenneth' and 'cabbage' get one point because they have one initial sound in common, while 'Peter' and 'peanuts' get two points, and 'Brenda' and 'bread', sharing /bre/, get three.

10.3   Innocence vs. sophistication

Strevens (1974) puts forward two principles of learning pronunciation. These are:

Principle No. 1
Most learners will learn to produce most sound features of a foreign language with reasonable accuracy by mimicry alone, given the opportunity; this ability tends to decrease with age.

Principle No. 2
Older learners can derive more benefit than younger learners from formal, specialized, intellectualized teaching methods; the more sophisticated the learner, the more sophisticated the instruction that can be used, and the higher the standard of achievement per hour of instruction he will typically reach.
(Strevens 1974: 185, 187)

▶   **TASK 104**

Where would you rank the following type of activity on an 'inncocence–sophistication' scale?

Which activities do you regard as most suitable for the specific learners you are likely to be concerned with?

- using head diagrams (so-called Sammy diagrams) for demonstrating and explaining the articulation of certain sounds
- watching feature films in the target language
- 'repeat after me', i.e. giving instructions to imitate and mimic certain sounds, words, or longer utterances
- using phonemic script to explain differences in pronunciation, for example of minimal pairs: /eɪdʒ/ vs. /edʒ/ for 'age' vs. 'edge'
- giving your students rules, for example, for the pronunciation of the English past tense marker *-ed* after different kinds of consonants:
  -ed is pronounced
      as /t/ after a fortis consonant other than /t/ (e.g. looked /lʊkt/)
      as /d/ after a lenis consonant other than /d/ (e.g. loved /lʌvd/)
      as /ɪd/ after /t/ or /d/ (e.g. hunted /hʌntɪd/, loaded /ləʊdɪd/)
- doing yoga breathing exercises to achieve muscular laxity in order to work on general features of pronunciation often referred to as voice quality.

Strevens (1974) emphasizes that teachers should take account of individual students and their learning ability in relation to age and degree of sophistication as a language learner. Generally speaking, techniques nearer the 'innocence' end of the continuum will often be sufficient for all types of learners to take care of most sounds to be mastered. For the remaining 'problem sounds', activities encouraging mimicry will usually be more appropriate for younger learners, while linguistically experienced adults are likely to profit more from cognitively orientated activities nearer the 'sophistication' end of the continuum.

Two more decisions which teachers of pronunciation usually have to take will, at least partly, depend on whether they judge an intuitive or an analytic approach to be more helpful for their learners. These decisions are whether or not to use phonemic script, and whether or not to give any pronunciation rules (an issue which we have also touched upon in the discussion of suprasegmental features).

As for phonemic script, textbook authors vary a great deal with regard to the extent to which they use special symbols. For instance, Gilbert (1993a) prefers to avoid them, and opts for symbols in bold capitals which are as closely related to English spelling as possible, such as the following:

A
Sibilants

Sibilants are sounds that make a hiss or buzz.

Voiced	**Z**	(buzz)	**ZH**	(measure)	**J**	(judge)
Unvoiced	**S**	(bus)	**SH**	(wash)	**CH**	(watch).

(Gilbert 1993a: 37)

Other authors, such as Bowen and Marks (1992), use a phonemic chart as the basis for many activities. They argue that an accurate and systematic visual representation of the phonemes of the target language can serve as a 'pronunciation syllabus' for the learners. They do warn teachers, however, not to overtax students whose first languages use non-Roman script.

 TASK 105

What do you think is the case for using phonemic symbols in your teaching situation?

Adrian Underhill argues for familiarizing learners with phonemic script, and mentions three abilities for which these symbols are important:

1 the ability to find the pronunciation and stress of any word in the dictionary
2 the ability to record in their own handwriting the pronunciation and stress of new words, phrases, etc.

3 the ability to objectify the string of sounds contained in a word and to
   study the sequences and clusters.

(Underhill 1985: 109, cited in Tench 1992: 97)

Paul Tench (1992) offers a discussion of 'Phonetic Symbols in the
Dictionary and in the Classroom' (his title) which will be useful to teachers at any level. He gives an overview of different transcription systems
and of relevant dictionaries, as well as specific suggestions as to how
these can be used in the classroom.

Linda Taylor's *Pronunciation in Action* (1993) offers several activities
for practising the use of phonemic script in a playful way, such as this
one:

22 Phonemic scrabble[1]

Level	Advanced
Students	Adults
Groups	Groups
Purpose	To improve students' knowledge of phonemic script
Text type	Phonemic scrabble board and tiles or cards

In this activity

Students play a board game to aid memorisation of phonemic symbols.

Preparation

The equipment you will need is a square-shaped board divided into about
20 × 20 small squares, and a pool of phoneme tiles or cards which fit the
squares. You will need one set for each group. The Sample teaching material
gives the symbols you need, and a frequency chart. Photocopy the symbols
onto card, making more cards for the frequent phonemes than you do for the
infrequent ones.

Procedure

1. Divide the class into groups and give each group a game board and set of
    tiles or cards. A list of phonemic symbols will also be useful (see
    Appendix 2).

2. Demonstrate the game with one group: Put all the phoneme tiles/cards face
    downwards on the table, and tell each member of the group to take a given
    number, unseen (seven tiles seems about right). The first player looks at
    his/her phonemes and tries to make an English word in sound (e.g. /si/ for
    'see'). If he/she can do so, he/she lays down this word on the game board.
    The next player looks at his/her phonemes and does the same, making the
    word fit in crossword fashion, as in the Sample teaching material for /mɪn/

(mean). The game continues in this way. If players cannot make a word, they pick up another tile/card from the pool.

3. Have the groups begin the game simultaneously.

4. After a given time, say twenty minutes, players count one point for each tile/card left in their hand. The player with the smallest number wins. Make sure you check the boards to see whether the words are all correct transcriptions of English sounds before declaring the winner.

Sample teaching material

Game board

A typical game board might look like the one below.

						w	e	n	z	d	eɪ
						ɪ			u		
			θ	æ	ŋ	k	s				
			ʌ				əʊ				
	k	æ	n				æ				
	w		d	r	ɪ	ŋ	k				
	s	i		ə			g	ʌ	n		
b	e	n	t				ə	m	ʌ	ŋ	
	t							t			
	l										
	d	u									

(Taylor 1993: 71–2)

What seems to be particularly effective about this activity is that in addition to being genuinely communicative, it forces learners to 'think in sounds'. This can be a very useful remedy against so-called spelling pronunciations—which is particularly important for English, where establishing the correspondence between written letters and spoken sounds is often difficult for learners. For instance, students may find it easier to pronounce weak forms if they can actually see the schwa-sound that they should produce in weak syllables, rather than the orthographic representation of the full vowel.

The schwa-sound can also provide an opportunity to discuss the question of the usefulness of rules. Again, learner types and preferred learning styles will normally be the most important criterion for teachers. But there are cases where it would seem a pity to deprive students of very simple guidelines: that schwa, for example, never occurs in stressed position. This rule will help learners with the stress pattern and pronunciation of most English words with two or more syllables.

▶ **TASK 106**

Can you formulate a simple rule for one or two other pronunciation points which might be helpful for your learners? If English is the language you are thinking about, try formulating a rule, with examples, for the distribution of clear and dark realizations of /l/ in RP.

The value of rules such as in Task 106 will also depend on the level your learners are aiming for. For instance, learning that in RP clear [l] occurs before vowels and dark [ɫ] before consonants or pause may be really important only for learners who want to sound native-like. On the other hand, it may be worth teaching most learners that /p/, /t/, and /k/ are aspirated at the beginning of a stressed syllable (for example, 'port') unless they are preceded by /s/ (for example, 'sport').

The debate among teachers about whether or not to give rules for pronunciation often centres around the value and feasibility of spelling rules. In English, for instance, there are hardly any one-to-one correspondences between sounds and letters. This makes any attempt to give rules for predicting sounds from spellings (or vice versa) a complicated task, definitely at the 'sophistication' end of the continuum mentioned above. A very useful reference for RP is Kenworthy's (1987) chapter 5, while for American English the authority to consult is Wayne Dickerson (for example, Dickerson 1992).

Closely related to the principles of 'innocence' and 'sophistication' is a distinction between what can be termed 'holistic' vs. 'discrete point' approaches to teaching sounds.

10.4 Articulatory settings

Most pronunciation teaching has traditionally concentrated on details, i.e. individual sound segments. However, strong arguments have been put forward for approaching pronunciation from the other end—from what is often called *articulatory setting* or voice quality. This involves learning to adopt the overall articulatory posture typical of the target language in order to get a general feel of pronouncing it. Adam Brown summarizes the advantage of this more holistic view:

'If a learner can be trained to abandon the long-term settings of his or her native language and switch to those of the L2 (to "get into gear", as Honikman (1964) called it), then this large-scale adjustment will facilitate small-scale changes needed in the articulation of the particular vowels and consonants of the language.'
(Brown 1992: 13)

Unfortunately, articulatory settings have not been studied extensively or systematically, and accordingly are ignored in most courses. However, a number of journal articles offer suggestions for teaching.

▶ TASK 107

Consider the following activities for teaching (about) articulatory settings and try out those which give specific instructions. Which seem feasible to you? What would you use them for? Sensitization? Production?

1 'One effective method of sensitizing ESL students to their own and each other's native voice qualities is to ask students to prepare a short phrase from everyday conversation, an announcement, or a tongue-twister to produce in their native language to the rest of the class. Even with only one or two representatives of each language, a linguistically heterogeneous class can yield noticeable differences. ... Students quickly learn that voice quality is not only individual, but also part of one's accent in a language.'
(Esling and Wong 1983: 293)

2 [instructions for obtaining an English articulatory setting:] 'taper and concave the tongue, draw it as a whole back into the mouth so that the pointed tip presses against the edge of the alveolar ridge; close the jaws, don't clench them; still the lips; swallow to relax; now limber up, repeat [t, d, n, l]'
(Honikman 1964: 285)

3 The teacher may ... demonstrate that it is perfectly possible to speak English with a pen-cap ... or other lightweight object placed lightly (not gripped) between the lips. Students may then be encouraged to do the same, and should be reminded that it is usual in colloquial English to use no greater degree of openness than the thickness of a cigarette or pen-cap. It is, of course, possible to do this in any language, but in English it is the norm; any larger opening is reserved for public speaking or moments of great excitement.'
(Jenner 1992: 43)

It will be evident from these extracts that suggestions for sensitization activities are easier to follow than the actual directions about what to do with the vocal organs.

Especially in the case of monolingual classes, a useful technique for sensitizing learners to how the native and target languages 'sound different' is to use what Bowen and Marks (1992) call 'bilingual minimal pairs'.

▶ ## TASK 108

Consider the procedure and rationale suggested for this activity. If you know a language other than English and German sufficiently well, try and devise such a list of 'bilingual minimal pairs' with reference to that language.

BILINGUAL MINIMAL PAIRS

2.4

LEVEL
Any

This activity is most obviously suited to monolingual classes, making use of contrasts between English and the mother tongue. However, it can also be used with multilingual classes, using one mother tongue or a mixture, and the point will still be made in a more general way.

FOCUS
Awareness of what is involved in learning the accent of a foreign language

Procedure

1 Put up on the board or OHP the list of minimal pairs. The example below is for German/English.

Vieh	fee	hier	here
putz	puts	Ei	eye
Schuh	shoe	Beule	boiler
denn	den	oder	odour
Föhn	fern	hau	how
vor	four	Bild	build
kann	can	Neuß	noise
Ahr	are	drei	dry
Gott	got		

© Longman Group UK Ltd 1992

MATERIALS
A list of *minimal pairs*, each pair comprising words from English and the mother tongue which have more or less the same pronunciation

TIME
10 minutes +

2 Tell the learners you are going to read down the list, but choosing only one word from each pair, either in English or the mother tongue. Ask them to identify which choice you have made in each case, by shouting out the language (in this case, 'English!' or 'German!').

3 Ask them to reflect on how they identified which language was being spoken. The discussion may well begin with generalities such as 'They sounded different' or 'Language X is softer, or clearer, or more musical', etc. This is fine as a starting point, but ask the learners to focus more on what was happening in the speaker's speech organs that was different for the two languages.

REQUIREMENT
You must be able to pronounce both languages well

(Bowen and Marks 1992: 21)

As Bowen and Marks point out, this exercise is meant to encourage learners to investigate general features of articulatory setting in different languages, 'i.e. typical distribution of muscular tension and movements of the speech organs which constitute the accent of a language' (Bowen and Marks 1992: 22). Differences learners might notice include the following:

– more or less tension in the neck, jaws, lips, or tongue
– more or less active use of the larynx
– differences of vowel length
– differences in degrees of lip rounding.

Bowen and Marks mention several other possibilities, the relevance of which will of course depend on the languages in question.

There is an alternative procedure for focusing on articulatory settings which is equally viable (and fun) in monolingual and multilingual classes. This is to ask students to devise a speech consisting of nonsense words, which they make up of sounds which they consider very typical of the target language. Laroy (1995) offers detailed instructions for such an activity, which he calls 'Reinvent English'—though in principle the procedure can of course be used for any language.

It has been customary in pronunciation teaching to concentrate on individual sounds and to practise them in isolation or in minimal pairs. In contrast, the argument put forward for starting with the articulatory setting is that this enables many learners to acquire new sounds more easily and, above all, to put them together and to make smooth transitions and links. Concentrating on this holistic aspect of pronunciation thus makes it easier to allow suprasegmental and segmental aspects to work in unison.

There is also a parallel between these arguments and insights into other areas of language teaching such as grammar and lexis, where the debate has been about how much conscious analysis should be required of learners. It has been demonstrated that it may be preferable, and certainly more akin to first language acquisition and use, to expose learners to a fairly large number of unanalysed holistic units, or pre-assembled 'chunks', such as 'on the other hand' or 'as far as I know'. Widdowson (1990: 91ff) gives a concise account of these arguments. Nattinger and DeCarrico (1992) is a full-length study of prefabricated language and its importance in foreign/second language learning, which also gives examples of such chunks in Chinese, Spanish, and Russian.

10.5 Individual sounds

Despite research findings that stress, rhythm, and intonation are generally more important for making ourselves understood, it is the individual sounds which, to most learners, seem to be the most readily perceptible, most 'tangible' aspect of pronouncing a foreign language: they can be isolated out of the speech stream and described much more easily than suprasegmental features. This conflict of priorities poses a problem for the design of pronunciation courses.

Judy Gilbert, for instance, reports that in the field tests for the new edition of *Clear Speech* it was found that students wanted individual sounds addressed first (Gilbert 1993b: vii). There will of course always be types of learners who are happy starting with suprasegmental aspects, such as many young learners, and wise teachers will take advantage of this opportunity. But if we acknowledge the wish of maybe the majority of older, more analytically minded students to give substantial coverage to sounds, there are a number of decisions teachers have to take as to the selection of sounds presented, and the most helpful progression for any specific learners. Possible criteria for selection and sequencing include the following:

- contrastive: problem areas predicted from a comparison with the learners' first language.
- frequency-based/functional: the 'work' individual sounds have to do in the target language in terms of distinctions in lexical meaning and grammar, termed *functional load*.

▶ TASK 109

Does one of these criteria seem to be more appropriate than the other with reference to any particular learners you are familiar with? Which conditions have to be met in order to enable you as a teacher to proceed according to this criterion?

Contrastive analysis
The idea behind a contrastive approach is that a comparison of the phoneme inventories of the learners' first language with that of the target language would allow difficulties to be predicted. According to the so-called Strong Contrastive Analysis Hypothesis (Wardhaugh 1970), difficulties will crop up where the two sound systems differ, where the target phoneme does not exist in the first language. To a certain extent, this approach seems commonsensical: we have all discovered a degree of systematicity in pronunciation problems which clearly stem from the fact that the target language makes distinctions between two sounds where the first language does not, or where there is a 'gap' in the first language system where the target language has a phoneme (see 2.2).

Obviously, such an approach will only be feasible in a fairly homogeneous class in which the students' linguistic background is not too varied. Also, teachers will require a sound knowledge of students' first language(s) and of the phoneme system of the target language—though just close observation will give a fair amount of guidance here. Many handbooks and teaching materials give lists of expected pronunciation difficulties according to learners' first languages: for example, Nilsen and Nilsen 1971, Baker 1982, Hooke and Rowell 1982, Kenworthy 1987, Swan and Smith 1987, Avery and Ehrlich 1992: chapter 8, Lane 1993, Taylor 1993).

▶ ## TASK 110

Unit 4 in Hagen and Grogan's pronunciation book *Sound Advantage* (1992) is entitled 'Troublesome Consonants'. It has the following headings:

Part I: /s/ and /z/

Part II: /θ/ and /ð/

Part III: /r/ and /l/

Part IV: Nonreleased Final Consonants [i.e. word-final plosives before a pause]

Part V: Consonant Clusters [such as /str/ and /ŋkθs/ in 'strengths']

Part VI: Consonant Combinations in Phrases and Sentences [such as /ndzgr/ in 'sounds great']

Bearing in mind your own first language if it is not English, or the first language of any learners you know, do you agree with Hagen and Grogan's judgement about what is 'troublesome'? Are there any consonants that you would want to add, or exclude, for *your* purposes?

Another factor which creates problems when basing our teaching on a comparison of first and second language phonemic systems is that phoneme *inventories* do not tell us very much about phoneme *realizations*. For instance, Arabic, Greek, French, English, Russian, Spanish, and Turkish have an 'r' phoneme, but these 'r's are realized in different ways: whereas the 'r' sound is voiced and continuous in most varieties of English, other languages prefer a trilled 'r' or an uvular 'r'. How much attention is given to such allophones in teaching will depend mainly on whether learners need to aim for near-native pronunciation.

It would seem, then, that knowing about differences between the phoneme inventories of our learners' first language(s) and that of the target language is an important factor in our decisions about the what and the how of pronunciation teaching, but it is not the whole story.

Frequency and functional load

As mentioned above, another possible criterion for the selection of sounds to be taught is frequency and/or functional load. The frequency criterion, which is also employed for vocabulary selection, can be used for pronunciation teaching by counting (and comparing) how often phonemes occur in running text of a specified length. In English, for instance, the most frequent consonant is /ð/, and the most frequent vowel is /ə/. Having established the relative frequency of phonemes in the target language, teachers may decide to give priority to frequent sounds while perhaps not treating infrequent ones. Charts of the frequencies of English phonemes can be found, for instance, in Gimson (1989) and in Taylor (1993: 74).

The functional load principle, on the other hand, does not refer to frequency in text, but to the number of words in which a phoneme contrast occurs in the whole lexicon of a language—in other words, how many minimal pairs are formed by a particular phoneme contrast. Catford (1987) illustrates this principle with reference to English:

'... the contrast between the English vowel [i] in *sheep* and [ɪ] in *ship* serves to distinguish many pairs of words (e.g. *peep/pip, peat/pit, peak/pick, peel/pill, peach/pitch*). The opposition [i/ɪ] has high functional load. In contrast, the opposition [u/ʊ] in *fool/full* distinguishes few pairs of words, and thus has low functional load.'
(Catford 1987: 88)

Brown (1988) also examines the notion of functional load and its applicability to pronunciation teaching.

Below is a table which lists the relative functional load of the following English phoneme contrasts: word-initial consonants, word-final consonants, and vowels in any position. Each of these three shows the contrast with the highest functional load on top (represented by 100). The remainder are represented as percentages of this maximum.

Table 1. *Relative Functional Load*

Initial Consonants	%	Final Consonants	%	Vowels	%
k/h	100	d/z	100	bit/bat	100
p/b	98	d/l	76	beet/bit	95
p/k	92	n/l	75	bought/boat	88
p/t	87	t/d	72	bit/but	85
p/h, s/h	85	d/n	69	bit/bait	80
l/r	83	l/z	66	cat/cot	76
b/d	82	t/k	65	cat/cut	68
t/k, t/s	81	t/z	61	cot/cut	65
d/l	79	l/n	58	caught/curt	64
p/f	77	t/s	57	coat/curt	63
b/w	76	p/t	43	bit/bet	54
d/r	75	p/k	42.5	bet/bait	53
h/zero	74	m/n	42	bet/bat, coat/coot	51

t/d	73	s/z	38	cat/cart,	
				beet/boot	50
b/g	71	t/tʃ	31	bet/but,	
				bought/boot	50
f/h	69	k/g	29	hit/hurt	49
f/s	64	t/θ	27	bead/beard	47
n/l	61	k/tʃ	26	pet/pot	45
m/n	59	b/d	24	hard/hide	44
d/g	56	d/g	23	bet/bite,	
				cart/caught	43
ʃ/h	55	v/z, d/dʒ	22	cart/cur	41
s/ʃ, d/n	53	b/m, g/ŋ	21	boat/bout	40.5
k/g	50	b/g	20	cut/curt	40
g/w	49	n/ŋ	18	cut/cart	38
n/r	41	p/f, s/θ	17	Kay/care	35
t/tʃ, d/dʒ	39	dʒ/z, m/v	16	cart/cot	31.5
s/tʃ	37	ŋ/l	15	here/hair,	
				light/lout	30
g/dʒ	31	p/b, m/ŋ	14	cot/caught	26
b/v	29	g/dʒ	13	fire/fair	25
w/hw	27	tʃ/ʃ	12	her/here,	
				buy/boy	24
ʃ/tʃ	26	f/v, f/θ	9	car/cow	23
f/v	23	tʃ/dʒ	8	her/hair	21
v/w	22	b/v, s/ʃ, z/ð	7	tire/tower	19
dʒ/dr, s/θ	21	θ/ð	6	box/books	18
dʒ/y	20.5	d/ð	5	paw/pore	15
d/ð, tʃ/dʒ	19	v/ð	1	pill/pull	13.5
t/θ	18			pull/pole	12
tʃ/tr	16			bid/beard	11
f/θ	15			bad/beard	10
f/hw	13			pin/pen,	
				put/putt	9
v/ð	11			bad/Baird	8
kw/hw	8			pull/pool	7
d/z	7			sure/shore,	
				pooh/poor	5
s/z	6			cam/calm,	
				purr/poor	4.5
tw/kw	5			good/gourd	1
tw/kw	5				
v/z	2				
θ/ð/, z/ð	1				

(Catford 1987: 89–90)

▶ TASK 111

Below are extracts from the tables of contents of two books for teaching (British) English pronunciation. Can you discern any relationship between the principles of frequency or functional load and the selection and order of the vowels presented?

Vowels

22	/ə/	a(gain)				
23	/iː/	see	/ɪ/	if		
24	/æ/	hand	/e/	egg		
25	/ʌ/	up	/æ/	hand		
26	/ɒ/	hot	/ɔː/	saw		
27	/əʊ/	home	/ɔː/	saw		
28	/uː/	food	/ʊ/	put		
29	/ɜː/	bird	/ɑː/	car		
30	/eɪ/	page	/e/	egg		
31	/eə/	there	/ɪ/	near		
32	/aɪ/	five	/ɔɪ/	boy	/aʊ/	now

(O'Connor and Fletcher 1989: 1)

Part 1 Vowels

Unit 2	The short vowels /æ/, /ɪ/ and /e/
Unit 3	The short vowels /ɒ/, /ʊ/ and /ʌ/
Unit 4	/ɪ/ & /e/ and /æ/ & /ʌ/
Unit 5	The long vowels /iː/, /ɜː/, /ɑː/, /ɔː/ and /uː/
Unit 6	/æ/ & /ɑː/ and /ɪ/ & /iː/
Unit 7	/ʌ/, /ʊ/ & /uː/ and /ɒ/ & /ɔː/
Unit 8	The long vowels /eɪ/, /aɪ/, /əʊ/ and /aʊ/
Unit 9	/eɪ/ & /e/ and /əʊ/ & /ɔː/

(Hewings 1993: iii)

When consulting textbooks which are structured by assigning units to sounds or sound groups, it may be helpful for the teacher to consider whether this selection seems to be based on a principle such as contrastive analysis (for monolingual classes) or functional load, or whether they simply reflect what is easy to name and describe: 'long consonants', 'plosives', or 'diphthongs' may be convenient labels for categorization, but they are often minimally relevant for pedagogy. The rationale behind proceeding according to principles, then, is to ensure the maximum 'yield' from your students' effort, by concentrating on likely difficulties (contrastive analysis) or on sounds which have an important function in the target language (frequency or functional load). For most purposes, though, a combination of these may be the best option.

▶   ## TASK 112

Consider the following activity for North American English from *Clear Speech* (Gilbert 1993a). Which rationale is it based upon, i.e. which of the above selection principles is it consistent with?

 More stops and continuants: grammar

A

Pair practice with R and D: past and present?

Pay attention to the verbs in the following sentences. If these verbs end in a stop sound, the sentence is in the past.

Student 1 says sentence (a) or (b). Student 2 says "past" or "present".

Example   Student 1: We shared all the food.
           Student 2: Past.

1. a. We share all the food.
   b. We shared all the food.

2. a. The dogs scare every cat.
   b. The dogs scared every cat.

3. a. Some speakers bore us.
   b. Some speakers bored us.

4. a. They hire new employees on Friday.
   b. They hired new employees on Friday.

. . .

(Gilbert 1993a: 16)

As Gilbert herself points out, 'this exercise introduces students to the fact that the final sound has grammatical meaning' (1993b: 11). In the sense that sounds are practised according to the 'work' they do in grammatical distinctions, for example, past–present or singular–plural, activities such as the one above can be regarded as an application of the functional load principle.

Sequence

Once the teacher has decided which sounds to work on, the question of sequencing arises. Here again, different authors take different views. The basic options are to work from what is most familiar, or to start with what is likely to cause the greatest difficulties. But these options do not need to be mutually exclusive, as will be evident from the following task.

► ## TASK 113

The technique suggested below by Bowen and Marks relates to the fact that different languages segment the vowel space in different ways (see **2.2**). Can you devise an analogous exercise which would be helpful for any vowels you or your students find difficult?

FINDING MISSING VOWELS

2.5

English has lots of different vowel sounds, and the task of learning to pronounce them all can seem daunting. Here, we suggest a simple strategy which uses vowels that the learners can already produce for discovering the articulation of ones they can't. For example, the learners can pronounce /iː/ (as in *beat*) and /uː/ (as in *boot*) reasonably well, but not /ɪ/ (as in *bit*).

LEVEL
Any

FOCUS
Articulating new vowels

MATERIALS
None

TIME
5 minutes +

Procedure

1 Ask the learners to pronounce /iː/, then /uː/, then a continuous sound that slides from /iː/ to /uː/. If they haven't done this before, it might take a bit of practice. Get them to stretch the sound over ten seconds or so.

2 What they need to do now is practise starting the same slide, but stop part-way along, isolating the sound they are making and pronouncing it without unnatural lengthening. If it sounds too much like /uː/, they need to go back; if it sounds too much like /iː/, they need to go further. With trial and error, they should be able to stop at the point where the slide passes through /ɪ/.

3 They will be able to use this strategy, as long as they need to, to rediscover the sound. They can then put the newly-discovered sound to work in words and more ambitious structures.

(Bowen and Marks 1992: 23)

The above technique can be very effective in helping learners to get a sense of an unfamiliar sound, i.e. where in the oral cavity it is produced. Most teachers would probably be intuitively wary of 'shocking' their students by concentrating on the most difficult sounds first. However, experimental research in speech therapy with children (Gierut and Dinnsen 1987) suggests that it may be most effective to teach second language learners first those aspects of the sound system which are most *different* from their first language. The assumption underlying this claim is that starting with the least familiar sounds will effect the greatest change in the learners' phonological system. The implications of these findings, if substantiated by further research, may well underscore the validity of teaching articulatory settings, as discussed in **10.4**.

10.6 Conclusion

It will have become obvious from the discussion in this unit that there are no right or wrong answers to the question of how to go about teaching the sounds of a foreign language. Decisions about whether to rely more on analysis or on intuition, whether to favour an analytic or an intuitive approach, how to select and order the sounds to be presented, will largely depend on the specific situation that learners and teachers find themselves in, the goals they define for themselves, and the conditions under which they operate.

The most important question to ask, however, is likely to be who our students are. We need to take the learners' perspective into account with regard to their feelings about pronouncing a foreign language, their needs, and their goals, and to help them appreciate the relevance of pronunciation to real-life language use. Of course these factors should not just determine the teaching of sounds, but of all aspects of pronunciation. But it may be that sounds are easier to teach in isolation, for their own (or rather, the teacher's) sake, and that it is in this area especially that teachers need to be reminded to make a real effort to integrate pronunciation with other aspects of communication. But the ability to make such efforts clearly depends on knowing *about* pronunciation as an essential feature of human language.

Exploration

11 Exploring pronunciation in your own classroom

In this section the focus is on ways in which teachers can explore and make use of the theoretical and pedagogic approaches to pronunciation described in Sections One and Two. The Tasks below are not intended as precise instructions for you to follow, but rather as suggestions as to how you might test out certain ideas against the reality of your own clasroom. In particular, you may have to modify activities to suit your setting and the kinds of learner you are teaching. If you decide that any particular suggestion, such as a certain extract, is unsuitable, it may be useful for you to reflect on *why* this should be so. The activities are, in principle, suitable for all levels of proficiency, except for a very few which are recommended for very advanced learners only.

▶ TASK 114

Aim
Self-reflection on how much attention you pay to pronunciation points in your teaching.

Resources
Pen and paper.

Procedure
For about a week, keep a diary of how often you cover pronunciation points (correcting, explicit teaching).

The following week, make a note of how often you feel you might usefully refer to pronunciation.

Evaluation
Is there a large discrepancy between the two diaries?

▶ TASK 115

Aim
To survey teaching materials for pronunciation points covered.

Resources
The general language coursebook(s) you are currently using, including the teacher's manual.

Procedure

Survey (several units of) the coursebook considering the following questions: are pronunciation points built in regularly? What aspects of pronunciation are covered—sounds, word stress, prominence, 'sentence stress', intonation, connected speech? Do listening tasks pay attention to pronunciation points? Is pronunciation integrated with the other material or is it 'tagged on'? Can you recognize a pronunciation curriculum at the side of the grammatical and lexical one—or is it even stated explicitly in the table of contents? Is pronunciation referred to in the teacher's manual, or in the introduction?

Evaluation

Does your coursebook have any clear strengths or weaknesses regarding the coverage of pronunciation?

▶ **TASK 116**

Aim

To gather data on your own speaking styles.

Resources

A tape recorder.

Procedure

Carry the tape recorder with you and record yourself in different teaching situations, with students of different levels, etc. If possible, also record yourself using the target language outside the classroom.

Compare the different extracts, listening in particular for rhythm, tempo, and clarity.

Evaluation

Does your speech differ noticeably in various situations? Which ones? Why/Why not?

▶ **TASK 117**

Aim

To explore the occurrence of connected speech phenomena in recorded course materials.

Resources

Tapes accompanying any coursebooks you currently use/have used in the past. Tapescripts, if available.

Procedure

Refer to 3.2.

Listen to several extracts from the tapes, evaluating them according to rhythm, tempo, and clarity. Make a note of the connected speech phenomena that occur.

Evaluation

Do the extracts vary in rhythm, tempo, and clarity?

Are connected speech phenomena frequent/infrequent?

Do the extracts attempt to imitate spontaneous speech?

Do the materials include unscripted (authentic) recordings?

How many different speakers? How many accents?

If there is little variation, what might you do to give your students more varied input?

▶ # TASK 118

Aims

To increase interest in pronunciation and to promote a meaningful discussion about it.

Resources

A questionnaire such as the one overleaf, from Kenworthy's *Teaching English Pronunciation*. (You can make up other questions which may suit your students better.)

Procedure

Discuss the questions with your students. If you teach a monolingual class, you may prefer to do this in their first language.

Evaluation

How involved did your students get in the discussion?

Did agreement or disagreement predominate, and what do you think are the reasons?

Were there questions which did not yield an interesting discussion? If so, why?

Are there questions which you would want to add?

If you are not teaching English: are there other questions which would be relevant in the context of your target language that you would want to include?

Questionnaire

1 Imagine you are talking in your own language with a foreigner. The
   person doesn't speak your language very well and is very difficult to
   understand. What do you do? Do you:
   (a) pretend you understand even when you don't?
   (b) ask him or her to repeat everything slowly and carefully?
   (c) try to get away?

2 What do you say when the foreign speaker apologizes for his poor
   accent? Do you:
   (a) tell him his accent is very good even when it isn't?
   (b) tell him that his poor accent doesn't matter?
   (c) tell him that his accent is very bad and that he must work hard to
       improve it?

3 How do you feel when a foreigner pronounces your name wrong?
   (a) very angry
   (b) it bothers me a little
   (c) it bothers me a lot
   (d) it doesn't bother me at all

4 How do you feel when you meet a foreigner who speaks your
   language with a very good accent?
   (a) surprised
   (b) pleased
   (c) not surprised
   (d) full of admiration
   (e) don't care or think about it

5 In the future, who will you speak English to?
   (a) mostly English people visiting my country who don't know my
       language
   (b) mostly English-speaking people in this country (Britain, USA, etc.)
   (c) mostly non-English people who don't know my language and
       whose language I don't know, so that we speak English together
   (d) don't know

6 Do you think it is more important to have good pronunciation when:
   (a) you are speaking English to English people?
   (b) you are speaking English to non-English people?

7 Below are some situations. When is it most important to pronounce
   well? Put them in order of importance with a number if you want.
   (a) speaking on the telephone
   (b) meeting someone for the first time
   (c) talking to someone you know very well (a good friend) in an
       informal situation (e.g. at a party)
   (d) doing business in English (e.g. at the bank, post office, bus station,
       railway station, in shops, etc.)
   (e) talking to strangers (e.g. asking the way)
   (f) chatting to a fellow student (e.g. during break time)

(Kenworthy 1987: 55–6)

▶ ## TASK 119

Aim
To create sensitivity to pronunciation points in students.

Resources
This task is feasible only with groups of fairly homogeneous first language background.

Make a tape of a speaker with a noticeable foreign accent in the learners' native language(s) (perhaps reading out a story). If possible, get a native speaker of the target language to do the recording for you. This has the advantage of reversing the usual roles of 'expert' and 'learner'.

Procedure
Play the tape. Ask students to make a note of any points they would like to point out to the speaker on the tape to improve intelligibility. Play the tape again.

Put students into groups to compare notes and to answer the following questions:

– Would you like to go on listening to this person reading the rest of the story?
– What is it that makes this person hard to understand?
– What should this person first pay attention to if he or she wanted to improve their pronunciation?
– If you met this person, would you tell them to do something about their pronunciation?

You might also want to use this as a starting point for a more general discussion on whether native speakers remark on learners' pronunciation, and in what circumstances.

Evaluation
How much discussion in and between groups did this activity generate?

Did your students turn out to be sensitive to minor points of non-native pronunciation of their own language?

▶ ## TASK 120

Aim
To learn to direct one's listening, consciously and selectively, to specific auditory impressions (much like directing gaze).

Resources
Variant 1
A piece of music with two solo instruments, for example, the second movements of J.S. Bach's concerto for oboe, violin, and strings (BWV 1060), or of the concerto for two violins and string orchestra (BWV 1043).

Variant 2

A tape of two speakers (one male, one female) reading the same text (a poem or narrative). The important thing is that their reading should be slightly staggered, i.e. one reader should start about half a second to a second later than the other (a technique sometimes employed in the theatre; we have also heard it used in a radio play).

Procedure

Play the tape to your students and ask them to listen to and concentrate on just one voice/instrument ('I am the oboe, you are the violin.'/'I'm the male speaker, you're the female speaker.') After listening, discuss with your students their perceptions, sensations, and difficulties. Then repeat the listening.

Evaluation

Did your students find it easy or difficult to concentrate on just one voice/instrument?

Did they find it easier the second time round?

Could you employ the same technique for focusing on certain aspects of pronunciation?

▶ TASK 121

Aim

To follow up perception as explored in Task 120 with production.

Resources

A poem translated into one or two other languages, such as the following 'English French German Suite' from Douglas Hofstädter's book *Gödel, Escher, Bach*.

Procedure

Only use languages which are spoken (not necessarily well!) by at least some of your students. Divide the class into three groups (or use just two languages and two groups if this seems more appropriate). Ask the different groups to read through their parts. Then ask the whole class to do a simultaneous performance of the suite, with all the language groups starting at the same time. It might also be useful to designate/nominate an observer group. This will probably generate a good deal of commotion and laughter. Discuss the experience with the class.

Evaluation

Were the students able to concentrate on their reading or were they 'thrown' by another group?

Did it take some groups longer than others to finish? Which language took longest?

English French German Suite

By Lewis Carroll . . .
   . . . et Frank L. Warrin . . .
      . . . und Robert Scott

'Twas brillig, and the slithy toves
Did gyre and gimble in the wabe:
All mimsy were the borogoves,
And the mome raths outgrabe.

   Il brilgue: les tôves lubricilleux
   Se gyrent en vrillant dans le guave.
   Enmîmés sont les gougebosqueux
   Et le mômerade horsgrave.

      Es brillig war. Die schlichten Toven
      Wirrten und wimmelten in Waben;
      Und aller-mümsige Burggoven
      Die mohmen Räth' ausgraben

"Beware the Jabberwock, my son!
The jaws that bite, the claws that catch!
Beware the Jubjub bird, and shun
The frumious Bandersnatch!"

   «Garde-toi du Jaseroque, mon fils!
   La gueule qui mord; la griffe qui prend!
   Garde-toi de l'oiseau Jube, évite
   Le frumieux Band-à-prend!»

      »Bewahre doch vor Jammerwoch!
      Die Zähne knirschen, Krallen kratzen!
      Bewahr' vor Jubjub-Vogel, vor
      Frumiösen Banderschnätzchen!«

He took his vorpal sword in hand:
Long time the manxome foe he sought—
So rested he by the Tumtum tree,
And stood awhile in thought.

   Son glaive vorpal en main, il va-
   T-à la recherche du fauve manscant;
   Puis arrivé l'arbre Té-té,
   Il y reste, réfléchissant.

      Er griff sein vorpals Schwertchen zu,
      Er suchte lang das manchsam' Ding:
      Dann, stehend unterm Tumtum Baum,
      Er an-zu-denken-fing.

And, as in uffish thought he stood,
The Jabberwock, with eyes of flame,
Came whiffling through the tulgey wood,
And burbled as it came!

Pendant qu'il pense, tout uffusé,
Le Jaseroque, à l'oeil flambant,
Vient siblant par le bois tullegais,
Et burbule en venant.

Als stand er tief in Andacht auf,
Des Jammerwochen's Augen-feuer
Durch turgen Wald mit Wiffek kam
Ein burbelnd Ungeheuer!

One, two! One, two! And through and through
The vorpal blade went snicker-snack!
He left it dead, and with its head
He went galumphing back.

Un deux, un deux, par le milieu,
Le glaive vorpal fait pat-à-pan!
La bête défaite, avec sa tête,
Il rentre gallomphant.

Eins, Zwei! Eins, Zwei! Und durch und durch
Sein vorpals Schwert zerschnifer-schnück,
Da blieb es todt! Er, Kopf in Hand,
Geläumfig zog zurück.

"And hast thou slain the Jabberwock?
Come to my arms, my beamish boy!
O frabjous day! Callooh! Callay!"
He chortled in his joy.

«As-tu tué le Jaseroque?
Viens à mon coeur, fils rayonnais!
Ô jour frabbejais! Calleau! Callai!»
Il cortule dans sa joie.

»Und schlugst Du ja den Jammerwoch?
Umarme mich, mein Böhm'sches Kind!
O Freuden-Tag! O Halloo-Schlag!«
Er schortelt froh-gesinnt.

'Twas brillig, and the slithy toves
Did gyre and gimble in the wabe:
All mimsy were the borogoves,
And the mome raths outgrabe.

Il brilgue: les tôves lubricilleux
Se gyrent en vrillant dans le guave.
Enmîmés sont les gougebosqueux
Et le mômerade horsgrave.

Es brillig war. Die schlichten Toven
Wirrten und wimmelten in Waben;
Und aller-mümsige Burggoven
Die mohmen Räth' ausgraben.

(Hofstädter 1979)

Did the students make any observations about the different auditory impressions the different languages produced?

Can you use these impressions for a discussion of articulatory settings?

Acknowledgement: the idea of having groups do a simultaneous reading in three languages comes from Barry Palmer.

▶ **TASK 122**

Aim
For the teacher: to find out which pronunciation points your students are already aware of. For the learners: to analyse somebody's pronunciation of the target language consciously.

Resources
A short tape (1–2 minutes) of a famous person speaking the target language as a foreign language, preferably with a heavy accent. This could be, for instance, a politician, an actor, or a sportsperson making a speech or giving an interview in your learners' target language. In most places there are radio programmes which offer plenty of opportunities to make such a recording.

Procedure
Tell students they will hear a short recording of somebody they know speaking the target language. They should pay close attention to the speaker's pronunciation: does he or she have a 'good accent'? What in the speaker's pronunciation strikes them as particularly good, or bad? In a more academically orientated course, you might hand out a listening sheet with categories and space provided for filling in examples from the extract, for example:

general impression	
clarity	
loudness	easy to hear _____ difficult to hear
speed	fast _____ slow
rhythm: chunking pauses	
individual sounds: consonants vowels	
word-stress	
prominence	
pitch movement	
any other observations	

Play the tape as often as necessary, then collect students' comments.

Evaluation

How easy did your students find it to name specific pronunciation points?

Did they find it easier to pinpoint segmental sounds than suprasegmental features? (If so, this is a convenient way to make them aware of the largely unconscious way we employ and process intonation.)

Did this activity offer you insights into which aspects are readily perceived by your students, and which ones they will need more sensitization to?

▶ # TASK 123

Aim

To explore the vital communicative importance of prosodic and non-verbal factors in pronunciation.

Resources

Dialogues, extracts from plays, and indeed any texts that can be interpreted in more than one 'mood'. For instance, different relationships between interlocutors may be read into one and the same dialogue, or a prose passage may lend itself to a 'serious' or an 'ironic' reading. There may be suitable passages in the textbook or other reading material you use with your class. If not, it is easy enough to write your own. Below is an example.

Version 1

A: a stern parent

B: an adolescent son or daughter

Sunday morning. B is asleep. The door opens and A walks into the bedroom.

A: (resolutely) Good morning, B.
   (reproachfully) It is 10 o'clock!

B: (bad-tempered) Morning.
   (cross) I was just having a wonderful dream.

A: (energetically) Look out of the window—fantastic sunshine, perfect weather for going cycling!

B: (disgustedly) Cycling? You must be joking!
   (contemptuously) I can think of something better to do.

A: (hurt) I bet you can—
   (reproachfully) What time did you get home last night?

B: (defensively) No idea.
   (resentfully) I didn't look at my watch.
   (flatly) What's for breakfast?

A: (sulkily) Kippers.

B: (sarcastically) Great!

B turns away from A and pulls the blanket over his/her head.

Version 2
A and B are a young couple, very much in love.

Sunday morning. B is asleep. The door opens and A walks into the bedroom.

A: (tenderly) Good morning, B.
(enticingly) It is 10 o'clock!

B: (brightly) Morning.
(entranced) I was just having a wonderful dream.

A: (enthusiastically) Look out of the window—fantastic sunshine, perfect weather for going cycling!

B: (teasingly) Cycling? You must be joking!
(amorously) I can think of something better to do.

A: (laughingly) I bet you can.
(with genuine interest) What time did you get home last night?

B: (casually) No idea, I didn't look at my watch.
(hungrily) What's for breakfast?

A: (triumphantly) Kippers!

B: (rapturously) Great!

B jumps out of bed.

Procedure
Prepare photocopies of the above dialogue or any text of your own, with identical wording but 'contradictory' stage directions.

Ask students to team up with a partner. Hand out version 1 to some pairs and version 2 to others. (If you use a prose passage requiring just one speaker, distribute your different versions to individuals in roughly equal numbers.) Ask students to rehearse the performance of their texts, as far as possible out of hearing of the others. Then ask them to perform for the class without announcing which version they are acting out.

If possible, make a tape recording of the performances.

After each performance, ask students to guess whether what they saw was a 'parent-and-daughter/-son' or 'lovers' sketch.

When you are through with the performances, discuss with the learners which features helped them identify the 'mood' of the different versions.

Evaluation
Did students find it easy to identify the different versions?

Were they able to pinpoint what made the crucial difference?

How much did the students rely on visual information (such as mime and gesture)?

When listening to the recordings, could you get them to home in on some of the interactional functions of intonation as discussed in 5.3?

▶ **TASK 124**

Aim

To explore practical examples of prominence, key, and tone; to integrate work on intonation with listening comprehension.

Resources

Some familiarity with the notions of prominence, key, and tone as discussed in 5.3 and 7.

Any recorded conversation you use for teaching listening comprehension; ideally the passage would contain a few examples of agreeing/disagreeing and a few tag questions.

Procedure

Briefly recap what you have said so far about the functions of tones (for example, common ground vs. new information), prominence (i.e. communicative salience), and key (high for contrastive, mid for additive, low for equative). You may of course choose to concentrate on just one of these phenomena at a time, in which case it would be best to start with prominence.

Play the recorded conversation to the class, with repetitions whenever required. Ask them to listen out specifically for the placement of prominence, instances of low key/high key, and proclaiming and referring tones. If working with advanced learners, you should be able to give them important insights into the way interlocutors tend to match their contributions in terms of key.

Discuss the learners' observations with them.

Evaluation

Which specific teaching points you were able to raise will obviously depend on your learners and on the material you used.

Were you able to exploit the material for intonation teaching which you might otherwise just have used for 'conventional' concerns of listening comprehension (such as vocabulary, functions, idioms)?

Did learners' observations lead to a discussion of how intonation is a means of negotiating topics and relationships between interlocutors?

Did a discussion arise about cultural aspects? (For example, directness/indirectness in disagreeing and the role that key plays in it, pitch ranges exploited in different languages, the need felt for using fall-rises as a mitigation device, perceptions of rudeness linked to high key, interruptions, etc.)

▶ TASK 125

Aim
To explore the notion of chunking into tone units through reference to words set to music.

Resources
Depending on what your students might be interested in and what is accessible to you, a selection of pieces of music with a strong 'language element', i.e. words set to music. These could be extracts from pop songs, folk songs, musicals, operas, oratorios, etc. Note, though, that it is important that the words should be easy to understand, and that they are not just subordinate to the tune. Recitatives from operas and oratorios are particularly suitable. Two songs with a strong narrative element (such as folk songs or ballads) could be compared. Similarly, extracts from recitatives in J. Haydn's oratorio *The Creation* (original in English) can be compared with less obviously narrative extracts from an opera. The pieces you can use will of course also depend on the target language in question.

Procedure
Familiarize learners with the notion of chunking in speech (as discussed in **5.1** under 'tone units' and **7.2**).

Hand out the lyrics of the pieces you want to play, and ask the learners to work in pairs, reading the lyrics out loud and marking them for chunking.

Play the pieces and ask them to observe whether their chunking is reflected in the phrasing, in the way the words were set to music.

Evaluation
Were learners able to recognize the phrasing in the extracts?

Did they detect discrepancies between their chunking and the phrasing chosen by the composer?

If you compared different pieces, was the phrasing in some more compatible with 'ordinary' speech than in others?

Did your students recognize that chunking may be a major factor for intelligibility and 'singability'?

▶ TASK 126

Aim
Heightening awareness of the frequency and quality of unstressed syllables, especially schwa.

Resources
A short extract of recorded speech (for example, a textbook dialogue); a transcript of the recording.

Procedure
This is best done in pairs or small groups.

Hand out the transcript and ask students to count the vowel sounds occurring in it (remind them that letters do not necessarily equal sounds).

Play the tape and ask students to listen out for how many of these vowel sounds are not pronounced in full—in other words, how many are schwa.

Compare notes in the plenary: roughly one third of the vowels of any text will be schwa.

Evaluation
Does the activity generate awareness of the sound-spelling relations of vowels?

How successful is it in generating awareness of the frequency of the weak vowels?

Do students notice that certain classes of words are always weak?

Does the activity generate discussion on what is stressed and why?

▶ TASK 127

Aim
To explore the notion that the regularity of stress-timing in English is truer for some texts than others.

Resources
A few lines of strongly rhythmic verse.

A short extract of radio news and/or a short extract of spontaneous speech; prepare a transcript of the recording(s) (2–3 lines are enough).

Procedure
In class, scan the verse and write out two or three lines using different-sized bubbles (oO) to mark stressed and unstressed syllables.

Hand out the transcript of the recording(s); ask students to decide where the stresses are by playing the tape as often as necessary. Do a bubble version of the listening text(s) and compare with the poem.

Evaluation
Is there a predominant patterning of stressed and unstressed syllables in the prose text(s)?

How does it compare to the verse?

What, in your opinion, is the value of rhythmical material for the teaching of English speech rhythm?

▶ # TASK 128

Aim
To raise awareness of the fact that the stress pattern is part of a word's identity.

Resources
Write a number of polysyllabic words on file cards, one word per card (for example, 'eternity'). Then do a second set showing the stress patterns of those words, again one per card (in this case, oOoo).

Procedure
Hand out one card per student in random order. Demonstrate with one example how to say the information on the cards aloud (for example, 'eternity' and 'laLAlala'). Then give them a minute to practise saying to themselves what is on their card.

Now ask them to walk around and find the person with the matching card without showing each other their cards.

Evaluation
Did your students find it easy or difficult to identify stress patterns?

Do you find this (sounds and stress together) a useful method for (a) revising words already familiar, and (b) the introduction of new items?

▶ # TASK 129

Aim
To improve sight-reading skills.

To test whether knowledge about sentence stress improves sight-reading skills.

Resources
(Sets of) two short reading texts (text 1 and text 2) of comparable difficulty.

Procedure
Record some of your students reading out text 1 unseen.

Prepare a teaching unit about stress distribution in texts to get across the difference between content words and function words. Students should understand that in sight-reading tasks it helps to look out for content words (nouns, verbs, adjectives) and to stress these in order to produce an acceptable version of a text they have never seen before.

Teach the unit.

Record students again as they read out a second unseen text.

Evaluation
In comparing the recordings, do you notice a difference in performance?

How readily did your students recognize the two categories of content words and function words?

Discuss with your students whether reading out text 2 felt different from text 1 (irrespective of your impression of the two recordings).

▶ TASK 130

Aim
To explore whether different modes of production have an influence on learners' pronunciation.

Resources
Tape recorder.

Two role play dialogues of comparable complexity, another role play in the form of role cards.

Procedure
Record several of your students reading out the first dialogue.

Hand out the second dialogue and ask them to learn it by heart. Then record the same students producing it from memory.

Third, record these students doing a role play from role cards.

Evaluation
Which of the three modes (reading, reciting, spontaneous production) brought the best results in terms of pronunciation for each individual student? Or was there no difference? Do individual students seem to have a favourite mode, or is there a general tendency?

The leading question: Do you think learning texts by heart can be a useful way of freeing the mind for concentrating on pronunciation?

▶ TASK 131

Aim
To explore connections between 'real world' concerns and selected aspects of pronunciation discussed in Section One (psychological, social, sounds, suprasegmental features).

Resources
The awareness and knowledge of certain aspects of pronunciation your students have gained from your course so far.

The following extract(s) from an article in the British newspaper the *Daily Mail* of 22 February 1992. It was printed next to a story about the arrest of a kidnapper after he had been identified from tape recordings of the telephone calls in which he demanded the ransom.

'CRUCIAL MISTAKE' WAS NOT DISGUISING VOICE ON THE PHONE

LANGUAGE experts pinpointed the kidnapper's crucial mistake as his failure to disguise his voice while making ransom demands by phone.

They said the rhythms, tone and dialect made it possible someone would recognise him.

Professor John Wells, Professor of Phonetics at London University, said: 'He didn't seem to be making any effort to disguise his voice. That was a major mistake – allowing himself to be recorded.

'He reacted to questions in a way that indicated he was using his real voice.'

Prof Wells said the voice had a number of 'very distinctive' characteristics.

He added: 'I think the great value of Crimewatch playing the recording was that people who had come into contact with him might have recognised the voice.'

Analysing the voice, he said: 'He is clearly a working-class Northerner. I don't think he comes from a big city.

'Giveaway'

Prof Wells, author of Accents of English, said giveaway words were his pronunciation of 'money' and 'telephone', whose open-ended vowels revealed he was from a small town or rural area.

His pronunciation of 'one', which most Northerners would rhyme with 'John', was also unusual, he added.

Forensic linguistic consultant Jack Windsor-Lewis, who listened repeatedly to the 170 words on the tape-recording, highlighted the man's pronunciation.

He said: 'It is an accumulation of many little things including the way he pronounces "i".

But he claimed the most striking feature was the man's way of speaking words ending in 'ing'.

And he added: 'He has a curious way of cutting it short although that could be the tension of the moment.

Mr Windsor-Lewis, formerly a lecturer in phonetics and linguistics at Leeds University, has been asked by detectives to make a more detailed study of the tape. He has suggested they should have it cleaned electronically to make it even more recognisable.

He added: 'He is a clear speaker, probably more intelligent than his class profile suggests. It is unvarnished speech, not giving himself airs. I doubt whether he has had access to higher education but I could be wrong.

'By elimination I placed the accent somewhere between Manchester and Sheffield and below Huddersfield.'

(Daily Mail, *Saturday 22 February 1992*)

Procedure

Ask your students to read the article and to list as many aspects of phonetics as possible which enabled the experts to identify the kidnapper from the tapes.

Evaluation

Was it easy or difficult for your students to perceive the relevance of phonetic knowledge to this real-world problem?

Did you discuss the mention of forensic linguistics, regional dialects, social judgements, vowel quality, and the very loose way in which certain terms are used (rhythm, tone, 'open-ended vowels')?

This activity could be followed up by playing short speech samples from people who are known to all your students (aquaintances, celebrities) and to ask them to identify the voices and then to explain *how* they knew who it was. You could do this activity first at the beginning of a course, keep records of the students' ideas, and then repeat it towards the end in order to see whether they can articulate their observations more precisely, i.e. how much declarative knowledge they have acquired.

Variation

With a very advanced class, you might like to use the following poem by Tony Harrison for much the same objectives.

Them & [uz]

for Professors Richard Hoggart & Leon Cortez

I

αἰαῖ ay, ay! . . . stutterer Demosthenes
gob full of pebbles outshouting seas –

4 words only of *mi 'art aches* and . . . 'Mine's broken,
you barbarian, T.W.!' *He* was nicely spoken.
'Can't have our glorious heritage done to death!'

I played the Drunken Porter in *Macbeth*.

'Poetry's the speech of kings. You're one of those
Shakespeare gives the comic bits to: prose!
All poetry (even Cockney Keats?) you see
's been dubbed by [ʌs] into RP,
Received Pronunciation, please believe [ʌs]
your speech is in the hand of the Receivers.'

'We say [ʌs] not [uz], T.W.!' That shut my trap.
I doffed my flat a's (as in 'flat cap')
my mouth all stuffed with glottals, great
lumps to hawk up and spit out . . . *E-nun-ci-ate!*

II

So right, yer buggers, then! We'll occupy
your lousy leasehold Poetry.

I chewed up Littererchewer and spat the bones
into the lap of dozing Daniel Jones,
dropped the initials I'd been harried as
and used my *name* and own voice: [uz] [uz] [uz],
ended sentences with by, with, from,
and spoke the language that I spoke at home.
RIP RP, RIP T.W.
I'm *Tony* Harrison no longer you!

You can tell the Receivers where to go
(and not aspirate it) once you know
Wordsworth's *matter/water* are full rhymes,
[uz] can be loving as well as funny.

My first mention in the *Times*
automatically made Tony Anthony!

Appendix

List of symbols/conventions

p	pen, copy, happen	ɪ	kit, bid, hymn
b	back, bubble, job	e	dress, bed
t	tea, tight, button	æ	trap, bad
d	day, ladder, odd	ɒ	lot, odd, wash
k	key, cock, school	ʌ	strut, bud, love
g	get, giggle, ghost	ʊ	foot, good, put
tʃ	church, match, nature	iː	fleece, sea, machine
dʒ	judge, age, soldier	eɪ	face, day, steak
f	fat, coffee, rough, physics	aɪ	price, high, try
v	view, heavy, move	ɔɪ	choice, boy
θ	thing, author, path	uː	goose, two, blue
ð	this, other, smooth	əʊ	goat, show, no
s	soon, cease, sister	aʊ	mouth, now
z	zero, zone, roses, buzz	ɪə	near, here, serious
ʃ	ship, sure, station	eə	square, fair, various
ʒ	pleasure, vision	ɑː	start, father
h	hot, whole, behind	ɔː	thought, law, north, war
m	more, hammer, sum	ʊə	cure, poor, jury
n	nice, know, funny, sun	ɜː	nurse, stir
ŋ	ring, long, thanks, sung	ə	about, coma, common
l	light, valley, feel	i*	happy, radiation, glorious
r	right, sorry, arrange	u*	influence, situation, annual
j	yet, use, beauty		
w	wet, one, when, queen		
ʔ	glottal stop (see glossary)		
	apartment [əˈpɑːʔmənt]		
	quite wrong [ˈkwaɪʔˈrɒŋ]		

In foreign words only:

x	loch, chutzpah	ø:	schön, Möbel
		/y/	buffet
		/y:/	grün

(adapted from Wells 1990)

*Neutralization

The opposition between /iː/ and /ɪ/ is neutralized and the symbol /i/ is used when the vowel occurs in a weak syllable at the end of a word. This sound is also used within a word when the i-sound in a weak syllable is followed by another vowel. The same applies to the /uː/—/ʊ/ opposition, which is neutralized to /u/.

Conventions for brackets

/phonemic transcription/
[phonetic transcription]

Glossary

accent: (1) variety of a language which differs from others in pronunciation; (2) social and/or geographical characteristics of the pronunciation of an individual speaker.

affricate: see **manner of articulation**.

allophone: different phonetic realizations of one phoneme, non-distinctive; often depends on sound environment; e.g. the /p/ in 'pot' is **aspirated** but the /p/ in 'spot' is not.

alveolar: see **place of articulation**.

articulation: the process of forming sounds with the speech organs.

articulatory setting: the overall posture of the organs of speech typical of a particular language or dialect (also called voice quality).

aspiration: puff of air following the release of a plosive, e.g. [pʰɒt].

assimilation: process of simplification by which a speech sound is influenced by the surrounding sounds (usually the sound following it) to make them more similar.

back-channel signals: agreement noises in conversation such as 'mhm', 'yeah'.

bilabial: see **place of articulation**.

Cardinal Vowels: set of universal reference vowels marking the extreme points of the articulatory space.

catenation: see **linking**; also called liaison; the last consonant of the first word is joined to the vowel starting the second word, e.g. 'get out'>'ge-tout'.

connected speech phenomena: cover term for several processes of sound simplification occurring in connected speech; see **assimilation, elision, linking, catenation**.

consonant: speech sound produced by creating an obstruction to the airstream during articulation.

consonant cluster: sequence of two or more consonants within one syllable, e.g. 'spreads' starts with the cluster *spr* and ends with the cluster *ds*.

content words: words which contribute to the lexical meaning of an utterance; usually stressed (nouns, verbs, adjectives, and adverbs of time, manner, and place).

contraction: actually a case of **elision**; mostly used of shortened forms of auxiliary verbs and negations, e.g. 'I will'>'I'll'; 'she is'>'she's'; 'will not'>'won't'.

deletion: see **elision.**

dental: see **place of articulation.**

dialect: a variety of a language differing from others in aspects of grammar and lexicon (and pronunciation); often used with negative connotation; strictly speaking, however, the standard is also one dialect of a language.

diphthong: a vowel sound where a glide from one vocalic position to another takes place, e.g. /eɪ/ in 'place'.

dominance: within Brazil's model of discourse, a dominant speaker has choice of who speaks when and what is spoken about; influences **tone** choice.

duration/length: (1) see **vowel parameters**
(2) one of the factors contributing to **stress** (prominence).

elision: process in connected speech by which a consonant sound is left out in order to make articulation easier, e.g. 'firstly' is pronounced [fɜ:sli] instead of [fɜ:stli].

floor: the right to speak.

force of articulation: the amount of muscular tension involved in the articulation of a consonant; **fortis** consonants (e.g. /p/, /t/, /k/, /f/, /s/) are **voiceless, lenis** consonants (e.g. /b/, /d/, /g/, /v/, /z/) are often **voiced.**

fortis: see **force of articulation.**

fossilization: an aspect (e.g. grammar, pronunciation) of a learner's language is said to be fossilized if, after many years of learning and using the language, it has reached a plateau, i.e. does not improve any more.

fricative: see **manner of articulation.**

function words: words which contribute to the grammatical meaning of an utterance but have little meaning in themselves, e.g. pronouns, articles, prepositions; usually unstressed; see **content words** and **weak forms.**

functional load: the use made of a linguistic contrast in the phonological system: the more minimal pairs a contrast between two phonemes distinguishes, the greater its functional load.

General American: the variety spoken by the majority of the population of the US who do not have a recognizably regional accent; also called Network English.

glottal stop: plosive produced by a closure of the vocal cords; used as an **allophone** of stop consonants in several English accents, e.g. 'apartment' pronounced as [əpɑ:ʔmənt] instead of [əpɑ:tmənt]; phonetic symbol: [ʔ].

intonation: 'speech melody', the use of pattern of **pitch** to convey different kinds of meaning in discourse.

intrusive 'r': a type of **linking** occurring at word-boundaries where two vowels meet (the first one often an 'a' or an 'o'-sound); a [r] which is not warranted by the spelling 'intrudes' to facilitate transition between the two vowels, e.g. 'law and order' [lɔːʳənɔːdə].

IPA: International Phonetics Association; also stands for the international phonetic alphabet standardized by that association.

key: relative pitch height on the first prominent syllable of the **tone unit**; speakers select from a three-term system to indicate particular meaning relationships between successive tone units: high key—contrastive, mid key—additive, low key—equative.

lenis: see **force of articulation**.

linking: process of joining one word to the next in connected speech, either by **catenation** or by inserting an extra consonant between two vowels, e.g. 'you and me' [juʷənmiː].

linking 'r': a type of **linking** where a silent 'r' from the spelling is pronounced to facilitate the transition between two vowels at word-boundaries, e.g. 'there is' [ðeərɪz]; applies only to accents of English where **postvocalic 'r's** are not pronounced otherwise.

liquid: see **manner of articulation**.

manner of articulation: of consonants: way in which the obstruction of the airstream is produced. The following are used for English consonant sounds:

Plosive (also called Stop)—the two articulators form a complete closure which is sudenly released (e.g. /p/, /g/).

Fricative—the two articulators come close together, forming a stricture through which the air can escape, thereby producing a hissing noise (e.g. /f/, /ʃ/).

Affricate—a sound where a stop articulation is continued as a fricative in the same place (e.g. /tʃ/).

Liquid—as for fricative, but the airstream has a fluid quality, thus less noise (e.g. /r/, /l/).

Nasal—as for plosive, but the closure is not released, the air escapes through the nose instead (e.g. /n/.

minimal pair: words in a language which differ only in one phoneme, e.g. pin–bin, lick–lock, lock–lot; frequently used for practising sound contrasts in a second language.

nasal: see **manner of articulation**.

paralinguistic features: those features of voice and body movement which accompany oral interaction, contributing to the meaning of the linguistic information.

phoneme: speech sound which is distinctive within the system of a particular language; see **minimal pair**.

phonemic script: a set of symbols for the transcription of spoken language; standardized by the International Phonetics Association (IPA).

phonetics: the study of human speech sounds; describes the wide range of sounds humans can produce.

phonology: the study of the use of the distinctive speech sounds (phonemes) in particular languages.

pitch: voice height; depends on the frequency of vibrations of the vocal cords; every person has an individual pitch range; relative pitch and pitch movement (tone) are made use of in **intonation**.

place of articulation: the location in the vocal tract where a particular speech-sound is produced; this is usually stated in terms of the active articulator (the part which moves) and the passive articulator (the part which is touched or approached/the part towards which the active articulator moves).

	active artic.	*passive artic.*	*examples*
(bi)labial	lower lip	upper lip	/p/, /b/, /m/, /w/
labio-dental	lower lip	upper teeth	/f/, /v/
dental	tongue tip	upper teeth	/θ/, /ð/
alveolar	tongue tip	alveolar ridge	/t/, /d/, /s/, /z/, /n/, /l/
post-alveolar	tongue tip	rear of alveolar ridge	/r/
palato-alveolar	tongue blade	alveolae/palate	/ʃ/, /ʒ/, /tʃ/, /dʒ/
palatal	tongue front	palate	/j/
velar	tongue back	velum	/k/, /g/, /ŋ/
glottal	two vocal cords		/h/, /ʔ/

(Brown 1993: 155)

plosive: see **manner of articulation**.

positioning of participants: the way interlocutors negotiate social roles and relationships in discourse (e.g. solidarity, dominance, shared knowledge). Suprasegmental features, notably intonation, play an important part in this.

postvocalic 'r': an 'r'-sound following a vowel; this is pronounced in some accents of English but not in others, e.g. 'park', 'where', 'here', 'cargo'.

prominence: the placement of stress in discourse by the speaker (often referred to as 'sentence stress'); see **stress**. Also known as highlighting, focus, tonic prominence.

prosody: often used synonymously with the term **suprasegmentals**, but may also include the study of **syllable** structure.

quality: see **vowel parameters**.

quantity: see **vowel parameters**.

rhythm: the sequence of strong and weak elements in language; there are different views: some say rhythm refers to the occurrence of stresses, others say that it depends on strong and weak vowels.

RP: Received Pronunciation, a social accent of English; Southern British Standard.

schwa: short, central vowel, neutral in quality; the first vowel in the word 'again', transcribed as /ə/; occurs in unstressed syllables only.

segments: individual sounds, consonants, and vowels.

semi-vowel: also called approximant or glide; extremely close vowel articulation which almost turns into a consonant, e.g. English /j/, /w/.

sentence stress: see **prominence**

stress: a syllable is stressed if it is pronounced with one or more of the following features: greater energy, greater length, higher pitch. Uses of stress: (1) lexical stress or **word-stress**; (2) prominence or 'sentence stress'.

suprasegmentals: features of speech stretching over more than one sound or **segment** up to whole utterances (e.g. stress, rhythm, pitch, tempo, voice quality); see also **prosody**.

syllable: a unit of pronunciation usually larger than a single sound and smaller than a word, e.g. the word 'syllable' has three syllables; there are one-sound syllables such as /ə/ in 'about' and one-syllable words such as 'pot'.

tone: see **pitch**.

tone unit: a group of syllables including a movement in pitch; used for description of intonation (also referred to as sense group, intonation group, tone group, or thought group).

toneme: in tone languages, distinctive pitch which distinguishes one word from another or two words consisting of identical **phonemes** from each other.

tonic syllable: the most prominent syllable of the **tone unit** where the main **pitch** movement takes place.

topic: what is being talked about.

variety: a social, geographical (or historical) variant of a language; neutral in terms of connotation, which the term **dialect** is not.

velum: the soft, back part of the roof of the mouth (soft palate); see **place of articulation**.

voicing: voiced sounds are accompanied by a vibration of the vocal cords, voiceless sounds are not; all vowels are voiced, consonants may be either. See **force of articulation**.

vowel: speech sound where the airstream escapes the vocal tract unobstructed.

vowel parameters: vowels are described in terms of how the chamber of resonance (the mouth) is modified. The two main features are: vowel quantity—the length of the vowel, e.g. short /ɪ/ vs. long /iː/; and vowel quality, defined by the movement of tongue, lips, or jaw, for example:

back vs. front vowels, e.g. /uː/ vs. /iː/
degree of lip rounding, e.g. /iː/ vs. /uː/
close vs. open vowels, e.g. /iː/ vs. /æ/

weak forms: the usual, unstressed forms of **function words.**

word-stress: a fixed pattern of stressed and unstressed syllables within a word, e.g. the difference between 'REcord' and 'reCORD'; see **stress.**

Further reading

Avery, P. and **S. Ehrlich.** 1992. *Teaching American English Pronunciation.* Oxford Handbooks for Language Teachers. Oxford: Oxford University Press.

Contains a description of the sound system of American English, a section on the identification of pronunciation problems of speakers of various first languages, plus a large number of classroom techniques for most aspects of pronunciation teaching.

Brown, A. (ed.) 1991. *Teaching English Pronunciation: a Book of Readings.* London and New York: Routledge.

A collection of articles which discuss major aspects of the field. Contains some classics.

Brown, A. (ed) 1992. *Approaches to Pronunciation Teaching.* London: Macmillan.

A collection of state-of-the-art statements on major aspects of pronunciation teaching.

Brown, G. 1990. *Listening to Spoken English.* 2nd edition. London: Longman.

A thorough and readable treatment of articulatory and perceptual aspects, paying particular attention to the difficulties of foreign learners when confronted with normal conversational English.

Catford, J. C. 1988. *A Practical Introduction to Phonetics.* Oxford: Oxford University Press.

This introduction to articulatory phonetics is exactly what it promises: practical. The articulation of sounds is explored by 'hands-on' exercises. Enables you to feel what is happening when you form sounds; mainly segmental.

Kenworthy, J. 1987. *Teaching English Pronunciation.* London: Longman.

A rich combination of reflection on, and practical ideas for, pronunciation teaching.

Roach, P. 1991. *English Phonetics and Phonology: a Practical Course.* 2nd edition. Cambridge: Cambridge University Press.

A step-by-step introduction to the sound system of (British) English. Covers sounds, stress, and intonation. Complete with exercises and tape, therefore also useful for self-study.

Speak Out! The journal of the International Association of Teachers of English as a Foreign Language PronSIG (Pronunciation Special Interest Group).

The only accessible, specialized, teaching-orientated periodical on English pronunciation teaching. Available from IATEFL, 3 Kingsdown Chambers, Kingsdown Park, Whitstable, Kent CT5 2DJ, England.

Wells, J. C. (ed.) 1990. *Longman Pronunciation Dictionary.* Harlow: Longman.

Gives the current most widespread pronunciation and alternatives for both British and American English. In addition, it contains useful notes on selected pronunciation points and guidelines for sound–spelling correspondences.

Bibliography

Abercrombie, D. 1965. 'Teaching pronunciation.' Reprinted in Brown 1991: 87–95.

Abercrombie, D. 1967. *Elements of General Phonetics*. Edinburgh: Edinburgh University Press.

Abercrombie, D. 1972. 'Paralanguage' in J. Laver and S. Hutcheson: (eds.): *Communication in Face-to-face Interaction*. Harmondsworth: Penguin, pp. 64–70.

Adams, C. 1979. *English Speech Rhythm and the Foreign Learner*. The Hague: Mouton.

Amis, K. 1954. *Lucky Jim*. Harmondsworth: Penguin.

Anderson, A. and T. Lynch. 1988. *Listening*. In the series *Language Teaching: A Scheme for Teacher Education*. Oxford: Oxford University Press.

Austin, N. J. and E. Carter. 1988. 'Nonacoustic contributions to the perception of fluent speech.' *Language and Speech* 31: 21–41.

Avery, P. and S. Ehrlich. 1992. *Teaching American English Pronunciation*. Oxford: Oxford University Press.

Baker, A. 1981. *Ship or Sheep? An Intermediate Pronunciation Course*. Cambridge: Cambridge University Press.

Baker, A. 1982. *Introducing English Pronunciation: A teacher's guide to Tree or Three? and Ship or Sheep?* Cambridge: Cambridge University Press.

Baker, A. and S. Goldstein. 1990. *Pronunciation Pairs: An Introductory Course for Students of English*. Cambridge: Cambridge University Press.

Barnard, G. 1959. *Better Spoken English*. London: Macmillan Education.

Barnes, N. 1988. 'Does intonation matter?' *Speak Out!* 3: 17 (Journal of the IATEFL Phonology SIG).

Batstone, R. 1994. *Grammar*. In the series *Language Teaching: A Scheme for Teacher Education*. Oxford: Oxford University Press.

Bolinger, D. 1986. *Intonation and Its Parts: Melody in Spoken English*. London: Edward Arnold.

Bolinger, D. 1989. *Intonation and Its Uses: Melody in Grammar and Discourse*. London: Edward Arnold.

Bowen, T. and J. Marks. 1992. *The Pronunciation Book: Student-centred Activities for Pronunciation Work*. London: Longman.

Bowler, B. and S. Cunningham. 1990. *Headway Pronunciation: Intermediate*. Oxford: Oxford University Press.

Bowler, B. and S. Cunningham. 1991. *Headway Pronunciation: Upper-Intermediate*. Oxford: Oxford University Press.

Bradford, B. 1988. *Intonation in Context*. Cambridge: Cambridge University Press.

Brazil, D. 1981. 'Intonation' in M. Coulthard and M. Montgomery (eds.): *Studies in Discourse Analysis*. London: Routledge and Kegan Paul.

Brazil, D. 1985a. *The Communicative Value of Intonation*. Monograph No. 8. Birmingham: University of Birmingham English Language Research.

Brazil, D. 1985b. 'Intonation in discourse' in T. A. van Dijk (ed.): *Handbook of Discourse Analysis*. London: Academic Press. pp. 57–75.

Brazil, D., M. Coulthard and C. Johns. 1980. *Discourse Intonation and Language Teaching*. London: Longman.

Broselow, E. 1983. 'Non-obvious transfer: on predicting epenthesis errors.' Reprinted in Ioup and Weinberger 1987: 292–304.

Brown, A. 1988. 'Functional load and the teaching of pronunciation' in Brown 1991: 211–224.

Brown, A. (ed.) 1991. *Teaching English Pronunciation: A Book of Readings*. London and New York: Routledge.

Brown, A. (ed.) 1992. *Approaches to Pronunciation Teaching*. London: Macmillan (Modern English Publications in association with The British Council).

Brown, G. 1990. *Listening to Spoken English*. 2nd edition. London: Longman.

Brown, G., K. L. Currie, and J. Kenworthy. 1980. *Questions of Intonation*. London: Croom Helm.

Brown, G. and G. Yule. 1983. *Discourse Analysis*. Cambridge: Cambridge University Press.

Butler, S. 1966. *The Way of All Flesh*. Harmondsworth: Penguin. (Originally published in 1903.)

Bygate, M. 1987. *Speaking*. In the series *Language Teaching: A Scheme for Teacher Education*. Oxford: Oxford University Press.

Catford, J. C. 1987. 'Phonetics and the teaching of pronunciation: a systematic description of English phonology' in Morley 1987: 87–100.

Catford, J. C. 1988. *A Practical Introduction to Phonetics*. Oxford: Oxford University Press.

Celce-Murcia, M. 1987. 'Teaching pronunciation as communication' in Morley 1987: 5–12.

Clark, J. and C. Yallop. 1990. *An Introduction to Phonetics and Phonology*. Oxford: Blackwell.

Cook, G. 1989. *Discourse*. In the series: *Language Teaching: A Scheme for Teacher Education*. Oxford: Oxford University Press.

Cook, V. 1968. *Active Intonation*. London: Longman.

Corder, P. 1981. *Error Analysis and Interlanguage*. Oxford: Oxford University Press.

Coulthard, M. 1985. *An Introduction to Discourse Analysis*. London: Longman.

Coulthard, M. 1992. 'The significance of intonation in discourse' in M. Coulthard (ed.): *Advances in Spoken Discourse Analysis*. London and New York: Routledge.

Couper-Kuhlen, E. 1986. *An Introduction to English Prosody*. Tübingen: Niemeyer.

Couper-Kuhlen, E. 1993. *English Speech Rhythm. Form and Function in Everyday Verbal Interaction*. Amsterdam and Philadelphia: Benjamins.

Cruttenden, A. 1986. *Intonation*. Cambridge: Cambridge University Press.

Crystal, D. 1969. *Prosodic Systems and Intonation in English*. Cambridge: Cambridge University Press.

Crystal, D. 1987. *The Cambridge Encyclopedia of Language*. Cambridge: Cambridge University Press.

Crystal, D. and **D. Davy.** 1975. *Advanced Conversational English*. London: Longman.

Currie, K. L. and **G. Yule.** 1982. 'A return to fundamentals in the teaching of intonation' in Brown 1992: 270–5.

Cutler, A. and **M. Pearson.** 1986. 'On the analysis of prosodic turn-taking cues' in C. Johns-Lewis (ed.): *Intonation in Discourse*. London and Sidney: Croom Helm, and San Diego, CA: College-Hill Press, Inc.

Dauer, R. M. 1983. 'Stress-timing and syllable-timing reanalyzed.' *Journal of Phonetics* 11: 51–62.

Dickerson, W. 1992. 'Orthography: a window on the world of sound' in Brown 1992: 103–17.

Doff, A. 1988. *Teach English: A Training Course for Teachers. Trainer's Handbook*. Cambridge: Cambridge University Press.

Ellis, R. 1994. *The Study of Second Language Acquisition*. Oxford: Oxford University Press.

Ellis, R. and **A. McClintock.** 1990. *If You Take My Meaning: Theory into Practice in Human Communication*. London: Edward Arnold.

Esling, J. H. and **R. F. Wong.** 1983. 'Voice quality settings and the teaching of pronunciation' in Brown 1991: 288–95.

Faber, D. 1986. 'Teaching the rhythms of English. A new theoretical base.' *IRAL* 24: 205–16; also in Brown 1991: 245–58.

Fairclough, N. 1989. *Language and Power*. Harlow: Longman.

Fry, D. B. 1958. 'Experiments in the perception of stress.' *Language and Speech* 1: 126–52.

Fudge, E. 1984. *English Word Stress*. London: Allen and Unwin.

Gardner, R. and **W. Lambert.** 1972. *Attitude and Motivation in Second-Language Learning*. Rowley, Mass: Newbury House.

Gierut, J. B. and **D. A. Dinnsen.** 1987. 'On predicting ease of phonological learning.' *Applied Linguistics* 8: 241–63.

Gilbert, J. B. 1978. 'Gadgets: non-verbal tools for teaching pronunciation' in Brown 1991: 308–22.

Gilbert, J. B. 1993a. *Clear Speech: Pronunciation and Listening Comprehension in American English*. 2nd edition. Cambridge: Cambridge University Press.

Gilbert, J. B. 1993b. *Clear Speech: Pronunciation and Listening Comprehension in American English: Teacher's Resource Book*. 2nd edition. Cambridge: Cambridge University Press.

Gimson, A. C. 1975. *A Practical Course of English Pronunciation: A Perceptual Approach*. London: Edward Arnold.

Gimson, A. C. 1989. *An Introduction to the Pronunciation of English*. 4th edition, revised by S. Ramsaran. London: Edward Arnold.

Gimson, A. C. and S. Ramsaran. 1982. *An English Pronunciation Companion to the Oxford Advanced Learner's Dictionary of Current English*. Oxford: Oxford University Press.

Grosjean, F. and J. P. Gee. 1987. 'Prosodic structure and spoken word recognition' in U. H. Frauenfelder and L. Komisarjevsky Tyler (eds.): *Spoken Word Recognition. A Cognition Special Issue*. Cambridge, Mass.: MIT Press, pp. 135–55.

Grosser, W. 1983. 'Interferenz in der Prosodie: Oberösterreichisch–Englisch' in A. James and B. Kettemann (eds.): *Dialektphonologie und Fremdsprachenerwerb*. Tübingen: Narr, pp. 235–54.

Guiora, A., R. Brannon, and C. Dull. 1972. 'Empathy and second language learning.' *Language Learning* 22: 111–30.

Hagen, S. A. and P. E. Grogan. 1992. *Sound Advantage: A Pronunciation Book*. Englewood Cliffs: Prentice-Hall.

Halliday, M. A. K. 1970. *A Course in Spoken English: Intonation*. Oxford: Oxford University Press.

Harrison, T. 1984. *Selected Poems*. Harmondsworth: Penguin.

Hawkins, P. 1984. *Introducing Phonology*. London and Melbourne: Hutchinson.

Hewings, M. 1993. *Pronunciation Tasks*. Cambridge: Cambridge University Press.

Hill, L. A. 1965. *Stress and Intonation Step by Step*. Oxford: Oxford University Press.

Hofstädter, D. 1979. *Gödel, Escher, Bach: An Eternal Golden Braid*. New York: Basic Books.

Honikman, B. 1964. 'Articulatory settings' in Brown 1991: 276–87.

Hooke, R. and J. Rowell. 1982. *A Handbook of English Pronunciation*. London: Edward Arnold.

Hornby, A. S. 1989. *Oxford Advanced Learner's Dictionary of Current English*. 4th edition. Oxford: Oxford University Press.

Hudson, R. A. 1980. *Sociolinguistics*. Cambridge: Cambridge University Press.

Hymes, D. (ed). 1964. *Language in Culture and Society*. New York: Harper Row.

Hymes, D. 1972. 'Models of the interaction of language and social life' in J. J. Gumperz and D. Hymes (eds.): *Directions in Sociolinguistics*. New York: Holt, Rinehart, and Winston.

Ioup, G. and S. Weinberger (eds.). 1987. *Interlanguage Phonology: The Acquisition of a Second Language Sound System*. Cambridge, Mass: Newbury House.

Jenner, B. 1989. 'Teaching pronunciation: the common core.' *Speak Out!* 4: 2–4.

Jenner, B. 1992. 'The English voice' in Brown 1992: 38–46.

Johns-Lewis, C. (ed.). 1986. *Intonation in Discourse*. London and Sydney: Croom Helm.

Kenworthy, J. 1987. *Teaching English Pronunciation*. London: Longman.

Kenworthy, J. 1992. 'Interactive intonation' in Brown 1992: 73–89.

Kreidler, C. 1989. *The Pronunciation of English*. Oxford: Basil Blackwell.

Ladefoged, P. 1993. *A Course in Phonetics*. 3rd edition (international edition). Fort Worth: Harcourt Brace College Publishers.

Lane, L. 1993. *Focus on Pronunciation: Principles and Practice for Effective Communication. Teacher's Guide*. London: Longman.

Laroy, C. 1995. *Pronunciation* (Resource Books for Teachers series). Oxford: Oxford University Press.

Laver, J. and **S. Hutcheson** (eds.) 1972. *Communication in Face-to-face Interaction*. Harmondsworth: Penguin.

Lehiste, I. 1970. *Suprasegmentals*. Cambridge, Mass.: MIT Press.

Levinson, B. C. 1983. *Pragmatics*. Cambridge: Cambridge University Press.

MacCarthy, P. 1976. 'Auditory and articulatory training for the language teacher and learner.' Reprinted in Brown 1991: 299–307.

MacCarthy, P. 1978. *The Teaching of Pronunciation*. Cambridge: Cambridge University Press.

McCarthy, M. 1991. *Discourse Analysis for Language Teachers*. Cambridge: Cambridge University Press.

Morley, J. (ed.) 1987. *Current Perspectives on Pronunciation: Practices Anchored in Theory*. Washington, D.C.: TESOL.

Morley, J. 1992. *Improving Spoken English: Consonants in Context. Vol. 2: Intensive Consonant Pronunciation Practice*. Ann Arbor: University of Michigan Press.

Mortimer, C. 1985. *Elements of Pronunciation. Intensive Practice for Intermediate and More Advanced Students*. Cambridge: Cambridge University Press.

Naiman, N. 1992. 'A communicative approach to pronunciation teaching' in Avery and Ehrlich 1992: 63–72.

Naterop, B. J. and **R. Revell.** 1987. *Telephoning in English*. Cambridge: Cambridge University Press.

Nattinger, J. R. and **J. S. DeCarrico.** 1992. *Lexical Phrases and Language Teaching*. Oxford University Press.

Nilsen, D. L. F. and **A. P. Nilsen.** 1971. *Pronunciation Contrasts in English*. New York: Regents.

Nolasco, R. and **L. Arthur.** 1987. *Conversation* (Resource Books for Teachers series). Oxford: Oxford University Press.

O'Connor, J. D. and **G. F. Arnold.** 1973. *Intonation of Colloquial English*. 2nd edition. London: Longman.

O'Connor, J. D. and **C. Fletcher.** 1989. *Sounds English: A Pronunciation Practice Book*. London: Longman.

Pike, K. L. 1945. *The Intonation of American English*. Ann Arbor: University of Michigan Press.

Poldauf, I. 1984. *English Word-stress: A Theory of Word-stress Patterns in English*. ed. by W. R. Lee. Oxford: Pergamon.

Ponsonby, M. 1987. *How Now Brown Cow?* Englewood Cliffs: Prentice Hall.

Porter, D. and S. Garvin. 1989. 'Attitudes to pronunciation in EFL.' *Speak Out!* 5: 8–15

Ratner, N. B. 1984. 'Phonological rule usage in mother-child speech'. *Journal of Phonetics* 12: 245–54.

Roach, P. 1991. *English Phonetics and Phonology: a Practical Course*. 2nd edition. Cambridge: Cambridge University Press.

Roach, P. 1992. *Introducing Phonetics*. Harmondsworth: Penguin.

Rogerson, P. and J. B. Gilbert. 1990. *Speaking Clearly*. Cambridge: Cambridge University Press

Sato, C. 1987. 'Phonological processes in second language acquisition: another look at interlanguage syllable structure' in Ioup and Weinberger 1987: 248–60.

Schmidt, R. W. 1990. 'The role of consciousness in second language learning.' *Applied Linguistics* 11: 129–59.

Schumann, J. 1975. 'Affective factors and the problem of age in second language acquisition.' *Language Learning* 25: 209–35.

Selinker, L. 1992. *Rediscovering Interlanguage*. Harlow: Longman.

Simpson, J. A. and E. S. C. Weiner. 1989. *The Oxford English Dictionary*. 2nd edition. 20 vols. Oxford: Oxford University Press.

Sinclair, J. and D. Brazil. 1982. *Teacher Talk*. Oxford: Oxford University Press.

Sinclair, J. and R. M. Coulthard. 1975. *Towards an Analysis of Discourse*. Oxford: Oxford University Press.

Skehan, P. 1989. *Individual Differences in Second Language Learning*. London: Edward Arnold.

Stern, H. H. 1992. *Issues and Options in Language Teaching*. ed. by P. Allen and B. Harley. Oxford: Oxford University Press.

Strevens, P. 1974. 'A rationale for teaching pronunciation: the rival virtues of innocence and sophistication.' *ELT Journal* 28/3: 182–9. Reprinted in Brown 1991: 96–103.

Swan, M. and B. Smith (eds.) 1987. *Learner English: A Teacher's Guide to Interference and Other Problems*. Cambridge: Cambridge University Press.

Swan, M. and C. Walter. 1984, 1985, 1987. *The Cambridge English Course 1–3*. Cambridge: Cambridge University Press.

Tarone, E. 1980. 'Some influences on the syllable structure of interlanguage phonology.' Reprinted in Ioup and Weinberger 1987: 232–47.

Taylor, L. 1993. *Pronunciation in Action*. Englewood Cliffs: Prentice Hall.

Temperley, M. S. 1987. 'Linking and deletion in final consonant clusters' in Morley 1987: 59–82.

Tench, P. 1992. 'Phonetic symbols in the dictionary and in the classroom' in Brown 1992: 90–102.

Trudgill, P. and J. Hannah. 1985. *International English*. 2nd edn. London: Edward Arnold.

Underhill, A. 1985. 'Working with the monolingual learners' dictionary' in R. Ilson (ed.): *Dictionaries, Lexicography, and Language*. London: Pergamon/British Council.

Vaughan-Rees, M. 1992. 'Rhymes and rhythm' in Brown 1992: 47–56.

Wardhaugh, R. 1970. 'The contrastive analysis hypothesis.' *TESOL Quarterly* 4/2: 123–30.

Wells, J. C. (ed.) 1990. *Longman Pronunciation Dictionary*. Harlow: Longman.

Wells, J. C. 1991. 'Phonology in EFL teaching' in R. Bowers and C. Brumfit (eds.): *Applied Linguistics and English Language Teaching*. London: Macmillan (Modern English Publications in association with The British Council). pp. 100–8.

Widdowson, H. G. 1984. *Explorations in Applied Linguistics 2*. Oxford: Oxford University Press.

Widdowson, H. G. 1990. *Aspects of Language Teaching*. Oxford: Oxford University Press.

Wolff, H. 1964. 'Intelligibility and inter-ethnic attitudes' in Hymes 1964: 440–5.

Wong, R. 1987. *Teaching Pronunciation. Focus on English Rhythm and Intonation*. Englewood Cliffs: Prentice Hall.

Index

Entries relate to Sections One, Two, and Three of the text, and to the glossary. References to the glossary are indicated by 'g' after the page number.

Acknowledgements

Extracts and figures from copyright material are reproduced by kind permission of the following:

Edward Arnold (Publishers) Ltd for adapted extract from *If You Take My Meaning: Theory into Practice in Human Communication* (1990) by R. Ellis and A. McClintock, and extract from *A Practical Course of English Pronunciation* (1975) by A. C. Gimson.

Cambridge University Press for extracts from *Ship or Sheep* (1981) by A. Baker, *Intonation in Context* (1988) by B. Bradford, *The Cambridge Encyclopedia of Language* (1981) by D. Crystal, *Teach English: A Training Course for Teachers* (1988) by A. Doff, *Clear Speech* (1993) by J. B. Gilbert, *Pronunciation Tasks* (1993) by M. Hewings, *Elements of Pronunciation* (1985) by C. Mortimer, *Telephoning in English* (1987) by B. J. Naterop and R. Revell, *Speaking Clearly* (1990) by P. Rogerson and J. B. Gilbert, and *The Cambridge English Course 1-3* (1984, 1985, and 1987) by M. Swan and C. Walter.

Daily Mail/Solo Syndication for article from the *Daily Mail* 22.2.92.

Harcourt Brace and Company for figure from *A Course in Phonetics* (Second Edition 1993) by Peter Ladefoged, copyright © 1982 by Harcourt Brace and Company.

Bryan Jenner and the Editor of *Speak Out!* for extract from 'Teaching pronunciation: the common core' by Bryan Jenner, first published in *Speak Out!* 4:2–4 (1989), Newsletter/Journal of the IATEFL Pronunciation Special Interest Group.

Longman Group UK for extracts from *The Pronunciation Book* (Pilgrims Longman Resource Books 1992) by T. Bowen and J. Marks, *Active Intonation* (1968) by V. Cook, *Advanced Conversational English* (1975) by D. Crystal and D. Davy, *Language and Power* (1989) by N. Fairclough, *Teaching English Conversation* (1987) by J. Kenworthy, *Sounds English: A Pronunciation Practice Book* (1989) by J. D. O'Connor and C. Fletcher, and *Longman Pronunciation Dictionary* (1990) edited by J. Wells.

Oxford University Press for figure from *Teaching American English Pronunciation* (1992) by P. Avery and S. Ehrlich, and extracts from *Headway Pronunciation (Intermediate)* (1990) and *Headway Pronunciation (Upper Intermediate)* (1991) by B. Bowler and S. Cunningham, *The Oxford Advanced Learner's Dictionary* by A. S. Hornby et al., *Stress and Intonation Step by Step* by L. A. Hill (1965), *Conversation* (1987) by R. Nolasco and L. Arthur, and extracts from 'Auditory and articulatory training for the language teacher and learner' by P. McCarthy first published in *ELT Journal* 30 (1976) and 'A rationale for teaching pronunciation: the rival virtues of innocence and sophistication' by P. Strevens first published in *ELT Journal* 28 (1974).

Peters, Fraser, and Dunlop for poem by Tony Harrison from *Selected Poems* (Penguin, 1984).

Teachers of English to Speakers of Other Languages Inc. (TESOL) and the author for table from 'Phonetics and the teaching of pronunciation: A systematic description of English phonology' by J. C. Catford in *Current Perspectives in Pronunciation* (1987) edited by J. Morley.

University of Michigan Press for extract from *Intensive Consonant Pronunciation Practice* (1992) by J. Morley.

Despite every effort to trace and contact copyright holders before publication, this has not been possible in some cases. If notified, the publisher will be pleased to rectify any errors or omissions at the earliest opportunity.